MEREDITH F. SMALL
KIDS

MEREDITH F. SMALL is a professor of anthropology at
Cornell University and the author of *Our Babies, Ourselves;
What's Love Got to Do with It?;* and *Female Choices.* She writes
frequently for *Natural History Magazine, Discover, Scientific
American,* and is a commentator for National Public Radio's
All Things Considered. She lives in Ithaca, New York.

Kids

ANCHOR BOOKS

A DIVISION OF RANDOM HOUSE, INC.

NEW YORK

Kids

HOW BIOLOGY AND CULTURE SHAPE
THE WAY WE RAISE YOUNG CHILDREN

MEREDITH F. SMALL

FIRST ANCHOR BOOKS EDITION, OCTOBER 2002

The Library of Congress has cataloged the Doubleday edition as follows:
Small, Meredith F.
Kids: how biology and culture shape the way we raise our children /
Meredith F. Small.— 1st ed.
p. cm.
1. Child rearing—Cross-cultural studies. 2. Child development—Cross-cultural studies. 3. Parenting—Cross-cultural studies. 4. Children—Cross-cultural studies. I. Title.
RJ47.S475 2001
649'.1—dc21
00-065684

Anchor ISBN 0-385-49628-1

Author photograph © Dede Hatch Photography
Book design by Gretchen Achilles

www.anchorbooks.com

Printed in the United States of America
10 9 8 7 6 5 4 3 2 1

For

FRANCESCA,

my kid

On the day you were born
the Earth turned, the Moon pulled
the Sun flared, and, then, with a push,
you slipped out the dark quiet
where suddenly you could hear . . .

. . . a circle of people singing with voices familiar and clear.

"Welcome to the spinning word," the people sang,
as they washed your new, tiny hand.

"Welcome to the green Earth," the people sang,
as they wrapped your wet, slippery body.

And as they held you close
they whispered into your open, curving ear,

"We are so glad you've come!"

—DEBRA FRASIER,
On the Day You Were Born, 1991

Contents

Kids

Introduction

"Parenting is the most important job of your life," my father once told me, "but one for which you get no training." He looked at me, one of his four children, and added rather sheepishly, "Most of the time, you fly by the seat of your pants."

I've thought about the seats of those pants a lot over the past few years, years during which I've been researching and writing about parenting across cultures and throughout human history and years during which I have been parenting my own daughter. In my research, I've questioned how we care for our children and why our styles of care are shaped a particular way. Is there a "best" way to treat a child? Might other cultures have ideas about parenting that make sense and be incorporated into our child-rearing practices? Can biology provide some answers?

And as a parent with anthropological training, I began to question seriously my own parenting and what my culture was telling me to do. Surely the way we treat kids in Western culture isn't the only way, or even the "best" way to go about this, I wondered. Slowly I began to question even the simple parenting tasks that I had taken for granted. Why do I expect my daughter to sleep through the night? Why do I expect her to be a certain height and weight and have a vocabulary of so many words at so many months? Why am I spending all my free time driving her to play groups just to expose her to other kids? What's with this concept of "timeout" parents have come up with and that ubiquitous phrase of encouragement, "Good job"? Deep down, I knew these were all cultural constructions. I wanted to stand apart and take a look at them—and their validity. Eventually, I just couldn't take on faith what the pediatrician said I should do to properly raise my daughter, or what Dr. Spock or Penelope Leach or Dr. Sears said was true, or what the advice books told me was "normal." I had to know the larger context within which such advice is given, where these pearls of wisdom come from culturally, and *why* exactly that particular advice is considered the "right" thing to do or expect.

In my previous book, *Our Babies, Ourselves,* I followed the work of a group of anthropologists, child development experts, and pediatricians who are interested in how various cultural styles mold parents and babies in their first year of life together. I learned that we adult humans are pretty nicely designed to take care of infants. Human babies are born highly dependent. When our human ancestors began to walk upright on two legs, this change in locomotion restructured the pelvis. This was not a problem at first, because our ancient ancestors still had infants with small heads. Until 1.5 million years ago, the ancestral brain was the same size as a chimpanzee's and could easily fit through the birth canal. But then came a push for large brain size. Adult humans have the largest brains relative to body size, and largest heads, of any mammal. But a pelvis designed for upright walking can't accommodate such a huge head. And so there is a compromise—our babies have had to come into the world a bit too soon, neurologically unfinished and unable to care for themselves. At the same time, adult caretakers come equipped with the ability to sense what babies need and they are compelled to engage in a physically and psychologically entwined relationship, a relationship that lasts for years, even a lifetime.

I also discovered that this relationship can play out in myriad different ways. Biology might dictate a close connection, but humans are highly flexible and so we interject culture into biology. In fact, in parenting as in all human behaviors, the dictates of biology are often ignored, denied, or overridden for all sorts of social or cultural reasons. The way we bring up our children, in fact, often reflects more about our social history and our folkways and our traditions than what babies and children might need and expect. And so I have become fascinated by that place where biology meets culture, the place where parents and their children are pushed by biology and yet pulled by culture.

Kids picks up where *Our Babies, Ourselves* left off. Once infants begin to walk and talk, a whole new universe opens up for them—and for us. The logical move for me, as a scientist, a writer, and a mother, was to follow along into that next stage. *Kids,* then, is an exploration of how biology and culture shape our kids, our parenting styles, and our expectations about this life cycle stage.

But why do this? There are the thousands of parenting advice books filling neighborhood bookstores and libraries full of academic studies in child development. Surely we have more than enough references to understand what makes children tick. After completing my research, I must answer: Maybe not. Most of that work is very narrowly focused—it deals primarily with white Western middle-class kids—and provides little context beyond what that restricted slice of modern society has to offer. Stand in front of all those advice books and ask a simple question: Where did all this advice come from? In most cases, it is based on cultural beliefs, tradition, and folklore, not on science. For example, advice about where and how long kids should sleep, how and what they should eat, or how to discipline kids is simply a set of cultural norms offered up as options. To caretakers, such advice in books or from the pediatrician sounds like the voice of authority, but, in fact, nonmedical advice is simply what that particular authority believes to be true. And that "authority" is just as much molded by his or her culture as anyone. Not all kids in the world grow the same, talk at the same developmental point, think the same, or act the same. Information about kids in other cultures shows how very different childhood can be across the world. Surely the millions of years during which the human species evolved also has something to add to our understanding of childhood. And so *Kids* provides a deeper and broader, and decidedly different, context for caretakers than the one provided by advice books, the pediatric medical model, or the academic discipline of child development. *Kids* is an attempt to go beyond the narrow confines of one culture, one socioeconomic class, and one species.

This book can best be described as the "anthropological" view of early childhood. What exactly do I mean by that? Anthropologists study humans: their current biology, their ancient history, and their culture. The anthropological view is one that is both deep in time, evolutionary and broad in scope, and that reaches across cultures. To understand humans as a species, we need both parts of that view; we need to know where we come from as a species and how we function as cultural beings.

The first part, the deep time or evolutionary part, can be gleaned from the fossil record and from other animal species, especially our close relatives, the primates. Studying them offers clues about our evolutionary history. Other mammals don't have childhood per se, for example. So why do humans have such a life stage? And *when* did this life cycle stage enter the human career? There are answers to both these questions in the bits and pieces of bones that our ancient ancestors have left behind and in the comparison to our closest relatives, the monkeys and apes.

An even richer context for childhood can be found by moving across the globe to other cultures. It's so easy to stay within the confines of one's own culture, or even subculture, to act as our peers do and think like everyone else. But what a revelation to look beyond our immediate circle and see that other people think and behave quite differently. Just about everything suddenly comes into question. Not all kids around the world go to preschool. Childhood in many cultures is a time of work, not play; older kids do the majority of child care and household chores. They carry babies, haul water, herd goats, and collect firewood. And they learn by experience rather than by sitting in a schoolroom or by reading a book.

The cross-cultural view shows that we in the West are rather insulated from what the majority of the world's population is doing during their early years of childhood. Our view of childhood is critically warped by a very recent economic affluence that allows most of our kids the luxury of play, school, and little responsibility. Other cultures teach us there are other ways to socialize, other ways to play, and other ways for kids to become moral citizens.

Kids begins in an American preschool—for what better way is there to capture the expected norm of early childhood in Western culture? In Chapter One, I then move to other cultures with a description of hunter-gatherer cultures and then a discussion of children who work. This far-ranging chapter should set the tone and the approach for the book—we will be traveling far and touching many bases. Chapter Two is the biological essence of childhood: Why do we humans have this extra period of life? I explain that we cannot take childhood for granted, because it wasn't always part of our ancestors' lives. Our ancestors, like all mammals, went from babyhood directly to adolescence; presumably our species, *Homo sapiens,* needed more. And so childhood has become part of the human career; as a result, the job of human parents is that much longer and more complicated. Chapter Three describes the fundamental job of childhood—to grow. What a miracle it is that we all develop from tiny helpless infants to functional adults in about eighteen years. Our bodies and our minds experience these biologically programmed changes the most during childhood. Chapter Four focuses on the other major development among young children—language acquisition. The hard-wired biological ability to talk and to understand the spoken word is something that defines us as human beings. More miraculous, acquiring language—this highly sophisticated and very complicated ability—happens most efficiently during childhood. Chapter Five wades more into the unknown—how kids learn in general and what we now know about early cognition. In Chapter Six, I move away from the individual and into society and follow kids as they begin to socialize and learn what it means to become members of the society around them. Their primate roots compel them to hang out with others, but they need to learn the cultural rules that guide "acceptable behavior," as well. Chapter Seven looks at gender issues: how boys and girls take on their sex-specific roles. I could not have written a book about children without somehow approaching the dark side of childhood—stress, child abuse, and violence. And so I do this in Chapter Eight. But my contribution is decidedly anthropological: What can evolutionary biologists and anthropologists tell us that might be useful for identifying kids at risk and then take measures to keep them safe? In Chapter Nine, I discuss the trade-offs we all face as we make parenting decisions.

Kids is not an advice book. It isn't a "how-to" book in any sense of the word. Instead, it is an anthropological view of early childhood offering a wider net than that provided by other books on children. I am not here to tell anyone how to raise their children. I only hope to encourage caretakers, and those who deal with kids in any way, to question what they do, to consider where their decisions come from, and to think about the fact that there might be other ways to guide our children into adulthood.

Opening our minds and hearts to a broader and deeper context about our children, and ourselves, can only make us better parents, better teachers, better citizens, and better human beings.

CHAPTER ONE

Kids' World

I'm sitting on a tiny blue plastic chair with my knees wedged under a very short table. My hands rest on my lap to stop any fidgeting while I wait for the midmorning snack of crackers, juice, and vanilla yogurt. The room smells of crayons, white paste glue, and kids.

Since this book is all about kids, I wanted to start by being a kid myself, if only for a few hours. I hoped to recall what life was like before I had to make a living for myself. I wanted a starting point for looking at kids in my own culture, not as a parent but from their perspective: What does it feel like to be a child in Western culture? What is the day like? How do they see the world? What's new since I was young? And so I've come to the Community Preschool at St. John's in Summit, New Jersey, to feel once again what it means to be a child.

The Community Preschool at St. John's is designed for three-

and four-year-olds from low- and moderate-income families. Director Susan Childs Merrick explains what makes a preschool different from day care: "We have a plan, and goals, and it's not just all unstructured play." The program is designed as a nurturing place where kids can express their creative skills and learn to be "confident, independent learners," as their school's brochure explains. This preschool offers early exposure to the structure of classroom, to the relationship between teachers and students, and how to get along in groups and to share. For many of the kids, Spanish is their primary language at home, and so preschool at St. John's is also designed to hone their English language ability before they enter kindergarten. And most of all, this place is just plain fun.

The hallway is lined with coat hooks placed three feet off the ground and a photograph of each kid hangs by bright yarn from the hooks, so that each child can easily identify where to hang his or her coat. There are two classrooms: one for the three-year-olds and one for the four-year-olds. You can tell which is which by the artwork on the walls—while handprints line the walls in the three-year-olds' room, more complex tissue paper wreaths, a skill of slightly older kids, adorn the classroom of the four-year-olds. Both classrooms are filled with supplies: Play-Doh and crayons, paints and paper, blocks of every shape and size. Everything is neatly stacked and labeled by the teachers, a lesson in order and place that distinguishes a classroom from a playroom.

I begin my morning with the four-year-olds. Clearly, they think it's pretty strange that an adult who is not a teacher is here to watch. At first, they glance at me out of the corners of their eyes as they file in, shifting their gazes quickly back to the teachers.

Teachers, in this preschool context, are not just authority figures, they are clearly trusted confidantes. Some kids skirt around me, some come up and ask my name, and a few quietly ask their teacher who I am. When teacher Molly Little tells them it's okay, then it's okay.

After an hour, none of the kids really care about me anymore, because they are busy, so terribly busy, as only kids can be. The morning starts with an hour of free play. If I were to choose, I'd go for the table spread with pinecones and leaves and take up the giant magnifying glass and check out everything at high power. But these kids know more of what the room has to offer. Three girls in the back of the room don aprons and set a table with plates and silverware and plastic food. A few girls and boys play with the wooden trains, making sure to add in the requisite *vrroom* noises at the right moments.

Soon all the kids are organized to follow Mrs. Little's lesson plan. They can make holiday wrapping paper or listen to a story. Later everybody has a snack and some rest time. At the end of the morning, they will head for the playground, where they will run around before their parents come to pick them up.

In the other classroom, the three-year-olds sit at tables full of puzzles and blocks, or pull on a red plastic full-body smock and paint at an easel. Their teacher, Alexis Staats, conducts a running conversation among these kids, questioning and answering, attending to the needs of each one. Along with her aide, Dina, she chats about their artistic creations or about the upcoming party. She tries to engage a boy who is running around the room. She seemingly has endless patience, as well as the ability to hone in exclusively on a single child a few moments before turning to another, like a good mother with brood of children who happen to all be the same age. I have a snack with the kids in this room too, which even the three-year-olds know is cheating since I already had one across the hall.

After a while, I settle down and take a deeper look at my surroundings, how it looks and how it feels. To my surprise, the whole experience begins to feel eerily familiar, as if cutting out a paper figure with blunt scissors or lying down on the floor with a blanket for a morning rest were part of my life only weeks ago. I am comfortable with the sense of a plan, the expectation that we would do this or that at such and such a time, that someone would lead and I would follow. More interesting, I find familiarity in the interactions among the kids: The interpersonal machinations it takes to socialize at four, I have to admit, don't seem all that different than socializing at forty. Three little girls sitting at the table painting and chatting could have been me and two friends at a bar—they too were gossiping about the behavior of another friend. Two younger kids negotiating a set of blocks remind me of adults sharing an office space or working on a memo together. I feel at home, even if the furniture doesn't fit.

But I am also trying to approach this preschool experience with an anthropologist's eye, and to do that I had to get beyond the idea that these rooms are just fun places to be in and on to the idea of classroom as cultural framework. No matter what is going on at home—and these kids are from all sorts of races, religions, and ethnicities—here they clearly experience a culturally Western sort of view, a culture that is industrialized and economically affluent, with particular rituals that have historical meaning. It just happens to be the Christmas holidays, for example, and so the kids are decorating trees, making presents, and inviting their parents to a holiday party. The decorations and party are nondenominational, but still, this is the time of year for celebration in the West, and the kids are encouraged to participate in some way or another. The toys, of course, are what kids in this culture play with—cars and trains and all sorts of kid-sized consumer goods that mimic what these children will want or buy as adults. And of course they communicate in American English, with all its idioms and dialects and rules for talking to teachers or to friends.

At a deeper level, what is valued in Western culture, how things are done and what is appropriate, can also be seen here. For example, the very concept of school, with a teacher as authority figure and kids at tables, would not be found in many third world countries. The idea of adults with no blood ties to these children having anything to say about what they do all day would be unacceptable in many cultures. And the classroom setting is a social system that is particularly Western—meeting new people that are not part of your family, cooperating, mastering new skills, and most important, learning to be independent and self-reliant.

In that sense, the preschool is a microcosm of the message Western culture in general sends as an imperative for a well-functioning society. One must be independent, self-reliant, but be able to cooperate and share and listen and obey authority. And these goals make sense both historically and economically—Western culture believes that the way to be successful is to be an individual achiever.

Such cultural molding, of course, goes on in some form or another for kids all over the world. It may happen in the family compound, in same-age play groups, or through community gatherings, but for all kids all over the world and throughout human history, there has always been a forum within which cultural values, traditions, and expectations are passed along. The content of the learning lessons, the different goals the cultures have, and various ways parents and other authority figures inculcate what is "normal" for that society is what's of interest. For Western culture, school and all it represents is a major player in teaching youngsters how to be good citizens. Such is the heavy hand of culture.

But cultural traditions are not the only level at which the morning could be analyzed. As a biological anthropologist who is interested in human biology, I also marked the developmental stage that I was witnessing. For instance, these kids were certainly conscious, and they communicated their thoughts and feelings well, but they obviously didn't have the mental comprehension of an adult, nor did anyone expect them to. They were also constrained physically—and not just by height. These kids were full of energy, running and jumping excitedly, but they often still slipped and fell. Their hands might hold a big color marker, but they surely didn't have the fine motor skills to do fine needlepoint. Beyond the cultural framework, the developmental biology of these kids struck me at every turn.

At the end of my stay, I was most impressed by the fact that kids are fundamentally a mixture of biology and culture; childhood, it seems to me, is a deeply furrowed path of developmental biology that constantly intersects with culture as children grow, physically and mentally.

That intersection of biology and culture during the childhood years is the framework for this book. And to begin building that framework, I start with a comparative question: What is a childhood like outside the familiar?

Children in Other Cultures

My images of children in other countries can be called up by trinkets that I have brought home from my travels. In my daughter's room is a shelf of dolls: African, Asian, and South American. They all wear some sort of "traditional" costume, bright skirts and strange hats, all representative of different lives. My favorite is the one from Zaire, a straw figure of a woman walking. She is holding an umbrella, shading herself and the tiny infant wrapped on her back from the sun. We also have an array of children's hats from Madagascar, because all Malagasy kids, from newborns on up, wear straw hats. And there are a few games, such as the pecking hen from Africa made from a wood paddle and weighted with a chunk of chewed aluminum foil. And some pictures of things I couldn't bring home—the bicycle made of wood that I saw on a back road in Tanzania, the dancer's costume from Bali—all wonderful creations made by or for kids. These artifacts can easily be enjoyed by kids no matter the culture—there is a universality in the fact that all kids like something new, something unusual to play with. But these articles all speak to something else—that every society or culture tries to mold their children in certain ways—and the artifacts of a culture often reflect this fact. The goods caught my eye not because they were like things we have at home but because they are different, and I wanted my daughter to get a taste of childhood in other worlds.

Those other worlds are so different because the people in them make a living (that is, stay safe, stay alive, get food, build shelter, and occupy their free time) in very different ways. As a result, the environment of care and the experience of children around the world varies.

Anthropologists have known this for decades. Margaret Mead was the first anthropologist to focus on children from other cultures. In 1925, she sailed to Samoa to study how children of the South Pacific interact with their world. Mead was seeking to support a theoretical agenda. She and colleague Ruth Benedict were founders of a school of thought called the Culture and Personality school that was bucking convention. At the time, scholars believed that people were the same the world over and that culture, or environment, had little influence on how people turn out. Mead and Benedict thought otherwise. They knew that the influence of culture would first play out in childhood and that groups around the world use the period of childhood to mold their kids into what it means to be an adult in their particular society. And so Mead was trying to document the process of how culture molds adult personality. In retrospect, this idea seems like common sense, but at the time, it was radical.

Thanks to Mead, and a legion of anthropologists who came after her, we have detailed accounts of children from birth on up from a number of cultures. Many of these ethnographies were recorded before these groups had had much contact with Western culture. As such, they now stand as records of the past, relics of a time before globalization. But many anthropologists who began their work before such cultures experienced much Western contact are still traveling to non-Western lands, and their work now records how many previously isolated societies are changing under Western influence and modernity. These ethnographies are ongoing and dynamic, and they underscore how people adapt to new ways. And they record how children, and the social construction of childhood, are part of that adaptation. This is not to say that what I present here is an unbiased sample of people around the world. By definition, I am limited to what ethnographers have collected. And their interests might not have focused on those issues of early childhood that would be most useful for this book. But taken together, a sample of kids around the world, in different cultures, different subsistence patterns, different ethnicities, belief systems, and ideologies, makes the point that ours is not the only kind of childhood that it is possible to have.

Kids at Play

Anthropologists have always been interested in people who make their living by hunting and gathering. For most of human history (that is, before ten thousand years ago when agriculture and animal domestication were developed and people settled down), everyone made a living by hunting and gathering. They might have lived in woodlands and gathered berries and hunted deer, or roamed across a dry plain and gathered roots and hunted antelope, but the method was basically the same—move across the landscape efficiently, picking up food as you go. People also lived in small kin-based groups, interacting with the same group of people for months at a time, perhaps meeting up with other bands that they knew well. Compared to how we live today, in villages and cities, it was a very different sort of social experience, one that few people today ever know. But, in fact, that's how our species spent 99 percent of our history. And so if we want to know where we came from, and perhaps why we act the way we do now, the lives of current hunters and gatherers might provide some clues about our biological and social design. And so anthropologists have turned to the remaining hunters and gatherers to glean some understanding about that lifestyle. In that sense, these people can also tell us something about the experience of childhood, how that life cycle stage was established, and how human kids behaved until very recently. In other words, following kids who belong to bands of hunters and gatherers might provide a window into what childhood is "supposed" to be like.

Interestingly enough, however, the story is not as clear as might be expected, and that's because even for hunters and gatherers, childhood varies among groups.

The classic record of a hunting and gathering community comes from the !Kung San people of Botswana and Namibia, Africa.[1] Until recently, when some San have moved onto settled areas, they lived on the dry savanna, gathering vegetable matter and hunting game. Since the 1950s, scientists have sought out the San, to record their lives and try to understand what it means to hunt and gather, at least in this particular ecological context. In 1963, a group from Harvard University decided to concentrate on one San group in the Dobe area and figure out how ecology (that is, land use and hunting) affects group structure.[2]

In *Our Babies, Ourselves,* I outlined infancy for the San—babies are carried at all times, fed on average every thirteen minutes, sleep at night with their mothers. Parents respond immediately to infant cries. In other words, the baby is part of a very dense social milieu and intimately connected to parents, family, and social groups. This caretaking package results in a baby that cries for less total time than the typical baby in the West.[3] More important, San parents believe that this caretaking package will result in an adult who will value what they value—social integration, mobility, and sharing. But what happens once these babies become toddlers? What happens as they enter early childhood?

Patricia Draper, a member of the Harvard contingent, took this analysis beyond the first year and concentrated on children in general.[4] She lived with the /Du/da[5] San, recording what children did all day and who they interacted with. She discovered that the way the San live is tightly connected, in a very real way, to the entire human life cycle. For the San, you simply can't separate life cycle from lifestyle. San children grow up among a very small number of people. When Draper was living with them in 1969, there were only sixty to eighty people in two camps in the area, although others might wander in at times. Draper writes of the "intimacy, closeness, and isolation" at the camps where members interact only with each other and rarely see strangers. As a result, San children know everything about everyone, and they conduct their lives in full view of every member of the camp.

The way the camp is constructed reflects this social intimacy. Although huts belong to each family, they are set in a circle with the opening facing inward. The structures are not really for living but for storing goods and sleeping in the heat of the day. The San spend all their time next to each other, rather than in their buildings. The camp itself is nestled into the bush; children venturing past the ring of huts are venturing into the outback, and so they seldom go beyond the huts. Draper says that children under ten always stay close to home and close to adults. At the same time, they have free range of the camp; there are no off-limits places or restricted areas. San children are simply part of the community, a community that consists of people of all ages. As a result, Draper explains, children interact with a variety of adults within the group over the years.

Also strikingly different from the Western norm, San children live and play in mixed-age groups rather than peer groups. For example, the average band might have only twelve children, maybe five girls and seven boys, and range in age from infancy to fourteen years.[6] That group is the play group and the peer group. There are no real team sports—it's hard to make a team with members who have such different motor skills. Interestingly, there is little competition among the children at all—they are wise enough to know the older ones will always win over younger ones, and since this is no fun, everyone cooperates. And there's not much problem sharing, simply because there are few material goods to compete over.

Draper found that very small children always seemed to be in a group that included an adult. In fact, in 173 spot observations of San children, she found no case in which any child was not in eye contact or within hearing of an adult; in only five cases was a child not in visual contact. In 70 percent of the times Draper checked, kids were actually in face-to-face proximity with adults. But these supervisors are not designated babysitters as such. They are simply adults finished with their work. Both San men and women have extensive free time—hunting and gathering take only a few hours per week and are done by different people on different days—and so some adults are always in camp to supervise kids. And there's not much to supervise anyway—there are no steps to fall down, no doors to hide behind, no traffic to avoid, and weapons for hunting are placed out of reach. According to Draper, the atmosphere at camp is always peaceful. Adults are very easygoing with kids. They simply assume children will be underfoot and are never cross.

San children are not expected to contribute anything to the camp. They don't help find food or participate in domestic chores. Kids might only be expected to fetch something for an adult if asked. In fact, Draper explains that San expectations are unusual in comparison to other hunters and gatherers in that girls reach fourteen years of age before they begin to gather, and boys turn sixteen before they hunt. In other cultures, children take on these roles much earlier. Even more surprising, older children are not responsible for caring for younger children, a normal practice in other parts of the world. But there is much less pressure to care for younger ones among the San. Since San women give birth only about every four years, the mother alone is usually able to care for each infant herself. She carries the child on gathering expeditions until it is two or three years of age. And when the mother elects to leave a small child back in camp, there are always a few adults to watch.

And so childhood for the San is like an idyllic childhood in the West—no responsibilities, no chores, all the time to play in the world. Could this have been the childhood of our ancestors? Is this the model of childhood that we might emulate?

Perhaps. But in a different part of Africa, another group of hunters and gatherers who have been intensely studied shows a very different picture of the early years.

In northern Tanzania, the Hadza people make a living by hunting and gathering over rocky terrain. They also traditionally gather wild honey and trade it with more settled neighbors for material goods, such as cloth and implements. Although some groups have turned to farming and attempts have been made by the government to settle the rest of the Hadza on farmland, the most recent surveys demonstrate that they still favor a life of wild game and native plants.[7] In general, their foods are much like those of the San, but the environment is less savannalike, so game and wild plants are more plentiful.[8] For example, Hadza men are able to hunt large game, such as zebra and buffalo, while San hunters rely more on small game, such as spring hare and dik-dik, tiny antelopes the size of slightly built dogs. Researchers estimate that there are approximately ten times as many trees where the Hadza live, and many of them bear edible parts. As a result, Hadza women don't have to travel as far as San women to collect enough vegetable matter.[9] Overall, the Hadza live in a food-rich environment compared to the San, a fact that is an important piece to the comparison of childhoods between the two groups.

Anthropologist Nicholas Blurton-Jones of the University of California—Los Angeles is in a special position to compare hunting and gathering societies. Having studied both the San and the Hadza, he has discovered that although both groups have a similar subsistence pattern, there are major differences between them, especially when it comes to children. Blurton-Jones found that the first year of life for Hadza babies is much like that for San babies—they are carried all the time, fed on cue (but not as continuously as the San), and everyone responds to infant crying, although parents sometimes ignore crying. But once past infancy, differences in childhood experience appear.

For example, Hadza kids are left behind in camp when they reach two years of age, while San toddlers usually stay with their mothers on gathering expeditions until they are much older. As a result, Hadza toddlers are weaned sooner, around two and a half years of age rather than age four.

When Hadza kids stay behind in camp, they become part of an unsupervised mixed-age group of kids that spends the day playing. More interesting, these kids often wander from camp on gathering expeditions of their own. Blurton-Jones describes how even three-year-olds will practice digging for roots, or picking up baobab pods, an essential food source for the Hadza, and process the pods for eating.

In contrast to the San, Hadza children are also regularly given tasks and chores to help adults. They might be asked to hold a younger child, or fetch water or firewood.[10] And unlike San parents who have infinite patience and never scold, Hadza parents reprimand their kids.

So in contrast to the life of a San child, Hadza kids have a more difficult life. Why is that? If parenting styles are tied to the economy and ideology of a society, and both the Hadza and the San are hunting and gathering communities concerned with group connection, why are the kids treated so differently?[11]

The answer, Blurton-Jones suggests, can be found in the fine details of childhood. The Hadza kids, it turns out, live in an area where they can fend for themselves. With lots of trees, lots of vegetation, and plenty of game, they can forage on their own and are less nutritionally dependent on adults.[12] Researchers estimate that San kids would have to forage much farther from camp, at least six kilometers farther into dangerous country where they might get lost, to gather the same amount of food that Hadza kids can get close to camp with little effort.[13]

How do the Hadza kids manage on their own? They are not guided, watched by adults, or supervised by adults. Instead, they act like a roving band of kids mucking about on their own. And this is normal childhood for Hadzas. Some learning takes place by hanging out with one's mother as she gathers, or father as he hunts, but the majority of the time, children learn about life from older children.

Perhaps what is most striking to Western sensibilities about children in hunter and gatherer societies is the fact that the multiage child group is an integral, normal feature of life. Kids are not sequestered into groups of peers as they are in America today, where the norm is to establish classes or play groups of same-age children, groups that are supervised by adults. We assume this is the best, and in fact the only way for them to learn. Yet not long ago, when many Westerners lived in small rural communities, when families were much bigger and each child had a number of siblings, children of all ages played together. In fact, age segregation is a function of our modern times when the birthrate is low and we have to organize our kids into groups. Have we, as a result, as parents, educators, and social scientists, misunderstood the natural setting for childhood learning?

And so children in hunter and gatherer societies teach us an important lesson. Children learn from other children, and it is normal for kids of all ages to play together. Younger children benefit from watching older kids, and presumably older children learn how to be responsible for those younger than themselves. Although Western affluence has given us the opportunity to provide our children with a rich childhood, we may miss the opportunity to belong to mixed-age groups of pals. This is a social legacy that we might benefit from, incorporating into our childrens' lives more often.

Kids at Work

"The kids work really really hard," anthropologist Karen Kramer told me from her office at the anthropology department at the University of New Mexico. The memory of her time in a remote Mayan village in the Yucatán peninsula of Mexico was fresh in her mind. "There are two things Maya kids never get yelled at for: making noise and getting dirty," she reflected. "But they do get yelled at to work." Mayan children start working at about three years of age, and by the time they are fifteen, Maya children are working as long and as hard as adults. They wash clothes, prepare food, haul water, and care for other kids.[14] Along with adults, they plant, weed, and harvest fields of maize. Boys and girls might take on different sorts of tasks, with boys doing more in the fields and girls doing the domestic chores, but both sexes work very hard. The overall time spent working is short when kids are very young, but it increases as they age, especially during the teen years. Grouping all the ages together, Kramer found that kids work about 30 percent of their day. Their contributions are clearly relative to their abilities, but much of Maya work is low-skill work and appropriate to kids. Because their work is a real contribution, the kids essentially pay for themselves and are not considered a burden, as kids are in the West. Large families are not an economic drain. "Children mature from being fully dependent on others to becoming economic participants and then net producers," Kramer explains.[15] This system has a clear evolutionary advantage, as children require less investment at every level, and they even give back to the economy of the family.

As Kramer pointed out to me, Western ideas about children and work just don't make sense among the Maya. And their system seems to work pretty well for them. After spending over a year living closely with the members of this village, she was struck by the overall level of happiness in the society. "They seem to be on the top of the curve for mental health," she commented. The way they treat kids, she feels, has something to do with the content-ment of the adults. "I am convinced they are doing this right," she told me. How strange that a society where children are expected to work, expected to add to the economy in very real ways, where childhood is not what we Westerners would call "idyllic" could be a society with a higher level of satisfaction than ours. Should we be reexamining the concept of "work" in relation to children?

What is work? One must ask. In the West, work is defined by payment, or some sort of compensation given to the worker. You perform a task and somebody gives you money in exchange. Our ideas about children and work are, of course, framed by the early years of industrialization, when children made up a large part of the factory labor force and were treated badly. In fact, labor laws were written at that time to get children away from work, to protect them from such harsh conditions. But aside from dangerous factory work, there are a number of jobs that kids can do and be responsible for on a regular basis, tasks that would not tax their abilities or put them at risk. For example, kids can babysit and help around the house with domestic chores. A more universal definition of work, and one that can be usefully applied to children, might stem from looking at the task itself rather than the payment or reward: Does that action somehow contribute to the household or the overall economy? Kids in the West certainly can do a number of household chores to help their parents and even free adults to have more time to work. More to the point, such work seems to benefit children. They feel pride in accomplishing a task, learn responsibility, and come to understand how to function better once they have left home and have to fend for themselves. Many children today no longer have chores. While this may be a sign of our affluence, we might be better off assigning children certain tasks to make them part of the functioning household and to help them learn what it means to be a responsible member of a group.

Around the world, most kids do work. Anyone who has traveled through East Africa probably has an image of the landscape etched on their brains: the endless savannas, the herds of antelope, the household compounds near the roads with wash drying on bushes, the kids in markets caring for other kids. Talk to anyone who has been a tourist in a third world country and eventually they will remark on one of the most startling visions of their trip—five- and six-year-olds hefting babies or with toddlers strapped on their backs. "I can't believe they make children carry their brothers and sisters. What are they thinking?" In the West, child care is the job of adults. Children are supposed to be free to either play or go to school. But our system is unusual. More often, child care in other parts of the world is done by other children. In a survey of 186 cultures around the world, researchers found that older kids, rather than mothers or fathers or other adults, are the primary caretakers of young children.[16] Odd as it may be for those of us in the West to hear this, in the majority of societies, "mothers are not the principal caretakers or companions of young children," as one researcher put it.[17] To be sure, infants until they are mobile at around one year of age, and often until they are weaned at two or three years of age, are the responsibility of mothers. But once those babies move into early childhood, again usually at one year of age, older children, usually siblings, are in charge. This system might result from economic necessity—mothers are often working in the fields or at markets and they need babysitters. But then why not use other adults? Instead, most parents have opted for child care by children, presumably because they believe that babysitting is an age-appropriate task. These children certainly learn parenting skills, and they have a great responsibility, including washing young children, carrying them around, feeding them, toilet training them, and keeping them out of danger. In other words, it's a job with responsibilities and expectations—and an important job. In fact, child babysitters are sometimes called "child nurses." And they are very good at their job. Cross-cultural studies show that seven-year-olds put in charge of two-year-olds imitate their mothers as they go about their duties.[18] They take on the high-pitched voice used by adults toward babies and carry them just as mothers do. And they are accomplished at keeping little kids out of harm.

More interesting, child babysitters make for a mixed-age learning situation for young children. In the West, we are so committed to the maternal-oriented style of upbringing that the thought of other kids as important players in the parenting scheme is so different that it is almost frightening. In fact, all child development research in the West, and all the theorizing about psychological development of children, especially Freudian models, are based on the belief that mothers are the primary, and hence most natural, caretakers.[19] But the ethnographic data places those assumptions in doubt. Perhaps, in fact, we should question the adult-child learning model and consider the benefits to kids and parents of integrating older children in our child-care system in a responsible way. In none of these other cultures are children totally left on their own—it's not as if the parents go off to work and leave an eight-year-old and a two-year-old in the house with no one else around. Instead, kids are part of a larger social group or household compound in which there is always some sort of adult supervision. Parents are usually within shouting distance, if not in visual contact, and other adults are around. Children and their charges are never really alone.

Although no one has documented how this type of child care affects the development of interpersonal attachments or adult personality, it is clearly a different sort of childhood.[20] From the older child's point of view, he or she begins to contribute to the family and can experience the sense of self-worth that comes with making such a contribution. Such children are less dependent than children in the West.

In addition to caretaking, children can also work around the household in other ways. Ruth and Robert Munroe and Harold

Shimmin conducted a systematic study of three- to nine-year-olds in four communities—Logoli children of Kenya, the Garifuna of Belize, Newars of Nepal, and kids in American Samoa.[21] They found that children as young as three years old had chores that took 10 percent of their day, and the percentage spent on tasks increased with age. By the time they are nine, kids in these cultures spend about a third of their nonschool time working. On average across these four cultures, kids work about 23 percent of their day at chores that aid the family. They fetch water, tend cattle and goats, clean pots, gather food, run errands, shop for food, and, of course, care for other kids. Not surprisingly, many of these tasks are divided by gender, as they are later between men and women. In rural Java, for example, girls cook, care for little kids, and prepare rice, while boys are responsible for collecting branches and leaves.[22] Sometimes they even bring in money. In Java, children earn wages by tending ducks, cows, and goats. These tasks are often fun for kids, rather than a hardship. Even in Europe in previous ages, children could sometimes earn small sums selling at markets or tending herds for others. Appropriate paid labor in those circumstances was a reasonable alternative to working around the home, where there is no monetary compensation.[23]

By some estimates, kids in other cultures essentially pay for themselves, as a result of the money they bring in, services they provide, and goods they produce, by the time they are seven years old.[24] Add to this the fact that when they grow up, children in these cultures tend to take care of their aging adults as well, and the result is a very child-friendly culture.

For all of human history, and presumably prehistory, children contributed to the household as they do today in most cultures around the world.[25] In fact, kids' work may have contributed to our very success as a species.

Most evolutionary theorists suggest that what makes human development different from other species is the highly dependent human child. Because children are so helpless, such thinking usually goes, they need both a mother and a father to form a pair bond and work together to bring up their offspring to reproductive age.[26] But anthropologist Anne Zeller, based on cross-cultural literature and interviews with ethnographers who have watched kids around the world, has zeroed in on the contributions children make to the household.[27] Childhood must not be a time of complete dependency, she reasons, but an arena in which parents can shift the burden of reproduction from one child to another. Once weaned, kids begin to do chores, run errands, and eventually care for younger kids, tend to the livestock, and work in the garden. Rather than being entirely dependent, they are helpers. Because of their kids' help, mothers are free to reproduce again. Given that, a long childhood in which an offspring is still attached to the household but of reproductive age might be an evolutionary *advantage* to a species in which babies need so much investment of time and resources. Childhood then becomes not a biological constraint but an asset, a fast track means of speeding up the human rate of reproduction. In such a view, it is an efficient behavioral solution to a biologically designed problem.

In other words, kids may be designed to work or contribute to the household. Perhaps this explains why my daughter, at eighteen months, loved to fold the laundry, sweep with her pint-sized broom, and pick up bits of paper and take them to the trash. She was, even at that young age, biologically designed and ready to make a contribution. I surely don't need her help. The adults in my house, with all our appliances, such as the washing machine and dishwasher, can easily do the work. But I encourage her aid, because it seems to me that she benefits from these tasks. First, she will learn how to cook and clean and to take instruction, all good skills. And perhaps more important, she becomes an integral member of the household: a contributor, not just a benefactor. And such simple chores, done together, makes us a family unit that not only plays together but works together. None of these chores are particularly difficult for her or for us, so they become little learning experiences and times of family interaction.

I began this chapter discussing my time in preschool because that is the most familiar early childhood setting for my own culture. In the West, we expect kids from about three or four years of age to be enrolled in some sort of institutionalized setting, interacting with peer groups and teachers, in an effort to improve the minds and skills of our youngsters. Day care, preschool, and kindergarten are the "normal" places for kids in industrialized cultures. This is a strange concept to close-knit societies where kids help with child care—to be sequestered with strangers, made to master and perform tasks that serve no obvious purpose, separated from the larger society. School is only a recent phenomenon in human history. Preschool is a mere blip in the history of human culture and seen in only a very few places today.[28] And yet most middle-class parents in the United States believe that going to school at three years of age is "normal," "expected," and the "best" way to educate and socialize our children. The cross-cultural information shows us that there are other ways for children to learn about responsibility and society.

No matter what ways kids learn and grow, they need this developmental time to mature and become functioning adults. Childhood is distinctive to our species; it is biologically scripted. Why is this true? When and how did childhood become part of our life course? What purpose does it serve? Such questions are increasingly the focus of anthropologists today.

CHAPTER TWO

The Evolution of Childhood

In late 1980, I spent fourteen months studying a group of Barbary macaques in a visitor park in southwestern France. I had worked on several groups of monkeys before, but this time instead of looking at the groups from outside a large cage, the monkeys roamed free across several acres, and I roamed with them. My project was to follow adult females and note their mating behavior. And so I spent all day walking among the monkeys. By the end of my time there, I knew them as well as I knew my own family. And I saw, and sometimes experienced firsthand, a raft of interpersonal problems and exchanges that were just like the problems and exchanges anyone has living in a group—disagreements, fights, individuals making up with each other, and social activities. I was absorbed by it all.

I was not allowed to touch the animals, but occasionally they touched me, sometimes in a nice way and sometimes as a threat if

I got too close. Often the worst offenders were young monkeys, which we classified as "juveniles." Just like human juveniles, they were full of energy and ready to have a good time. There were twenty-three of them that year, all born in the fall two years previously, hanging out together as a group. It's a great age for a macaque—they're fully weaned but still connected to their mothers and not yet ready for adult life. The following year, at three years old, the females would be experiencing their first mating season and the males would start learning the status games of adult males. But for several months, they were free to look for trouble. And they often looked to me.

They had the most fun when it rained. I'd be wearing a green plastic poncho and following an adult female, for example, setting the timer I used to pace the observations and sneaking a hand under a plastic bag to record her behavior on paper, concentrating on the task at hand. Suddenly, I'd feel the *thwack* of a small body hurled against my back—a juvenile had jumped from God knows where onto the poncho, grabbing frantically with tiny hands as he or she slid to the ground. Soon it became a game of king of the hill, and one after another, small monkeys mounted my back, crawled to my shoulders, and slid down either side of my body. Sometimes I'd twist and turn to get them off, knowing I must keep my scientific distance intact. But they'd have none of that. *Thwack,* slide, *thwack,* slide.

I remember the day in the summer when, as I was resting quietly on a low wall, a juvenile jumped into my lap, looked curiously at his reflection in my sunglasses, grabbed my nose in his tiny clammy fingers, and gave it a good twist. If monkeys could laugh, I'm sure he would have.

Although I remember these juveniles well and had a great deal of contact with them, they were not the focus of my studies, so I tended to push my observations of them to the back of my mind. In fact, none of them yet had been marked with the artificial dye used by the park staff for individual identification, and I had spent no time looking at them as individuals. As a result, they all looked alike to me. In fact, they often seemed like a wild horde, wreaking monkey havoc wherever they went. Those of us who worked at the park used to refer to them as "those damn kids," or the "terrible twos," who were stealing our pens and pulling our hair. We forgot, as most adults do, to sit down and take those juveniles seriously.

And we should have, because our impression of their place in monkey society was quite wrong. Although scientists are just beginning to work on this life cycle stage, they are finding that nonhuman primate juveniles live an accelerated life relative to human primates.[1] Once weaned (and time to weaning varies with species), they are extremely independent compared to humans at the same developmental stage. Their mothers are still around, and they go to her when they are in trouble, and sleep with her at night, but during the day, these youngsters are relatively on their own. They don't depend on their mothers for food, for example. More startling, nonhuman primates very swiftly move from weanlings that are still somewhat attached to their mothers to subadults ready to mate. The time from weaning to maturity for female macaques is only one or two years. In other words, nonhuman primates start as infants, become independent juveniles, and then become adults— they are never children.

Childhood is unique to the human species. Beyond social constructions, there are real biological markers of human childhood.

Other animals, even other primates, just don't have them. And yet this is such a critical time for humans that natural selection must have favored the appearance of this stage.

So where did human childhood come from? And why, in the evolutionary sense, is it here?

Why Childhood?

Children are small people, unable to communicate in sophisticated ways. They seem to need constant care and attention. When dealing with the demands of young children, most of us forget they are simply less mature versions of ourselves and that each of us also went through this developmental stage. And yet only humans *have* childhood. Other animals have babies, they have offspring, but they do not have children. How can this be?

A mouse, for example, is born and twenty days later it is weaned and soon able to reproduce.[2] These animals go directly and rather swiftly from being dependent infants to independent adults. Social animals, such as wolves, dolphins, elephants, and primates, animals with larger brains and longer lives, have a somewhat different life cycle. Besides infancy and adulthood, they also have a stage called "juvenile." This is a preadolescent stage during which these animals are capable of feeding themselves but they are not yet reproductively active. The life cycle of other big-brained social species can therefore be divided into infant, juvenile, subadult, and then adult. Even so, other animals seem to have fewer life cycle stages than humans.

Humans, like the long-lived, larger-brained, and highly social types of animals, spend some time as juveniles. But humans go further in adjusting the life cycle. After infancy (from birth to one year), we have childhood, a stage that runs from ages one to six. Juveniles are young children aged six through ten, adolescents aged eleven through eighteen, and then we become adults. Nor are these stages a mere matter of semantics. There are physical and behavioral markers for each of these stages: Each level, in and of itself, is a separate physiological and behavioral category that can be defined. Infants suckle from their mothers, children are weaned but still physically dependent and need to be fed, juveniles are food dependent but physically independent, adolescents are sexually mature, and adults are on their own.

Various researchers define the age of human childhood in different ways. Some feel childhood begins at weaning, when babies move from breast milk to solid food; they suggest childhood ends around seven years of age.[3] Since, in most cultures, weaning begins between two and three years of age, childhood under this definition would officially begin at this point. UNICEF, on the other hand, defines childhood as birth to age fifteen; their definition is a policy decision, as it helps set their agenda to help all youngsters. Others feel that it is impossible to pin down the exact age limits of the childhood stage, because the experience is so different, depending on the culture—childhood can, for example, be abruptly interrupted by war or disease, when children are forced to mature before their time.[4] No one is precisely sure where to draw the lines around childhood. At one end of the spectrum, childhood could be defined as the period from three years of age to, say, seven; and at the other end, it could span ages one to ten.

In a sense, the fuzzy age span of childhood makes it a more interesting stage to investigate. This is the stage that is not only highly variable at the biological level in terms of interindividual development, it is also the stage where environment—and by that I mean the family niche and greater social circle—has a profound influence. And kids themselves seek that interaction. During the first year of life, infants need care more than anything else; but once babies begin to walk and explore the world a bit on their own, it's a whole new ball game. They choose to go here or there, they choose to pick up this or that. They become mental and emotional sponges, open to the world. And so the move into childhood, beginning at one or two or three years of age, is the transition from total dependence on adults toward a youngster who walks, talks, interacts socially, and understands the world around him or her. And it ends when the body begins to mature sexually.

No matter how you define it, childhood is a period that lasts anywhere from four to eight years—longer than infancy, the juvenile stage, or adolescence. And how odd it is that only humans have this extended period.

Are Humans Special?

Humans, of course, are animals. Sometimes we forget this basic fact of biology, but our species evolved by natural selection just like all other animals. We are born, live, eat, eliminate, sleep, interact, mate, bear young, and die, just like all other creatures on Earth. Like other mammals, we give birth to live young, we have hair on our bodies rather than feathers, and we keep a steady internal body temperature. Like other primates, those of our taxonomic order, we are social animals, have big brains compared to other mammals, and care extensively for our young. There are also special things about being human, just as there are special things about any particular species. We reason, puzzle-solve, rely on culture to get by, and we are highly self-conscious.

Some think these special attributes put us above other creatures, but in the end, we all die just like any other organic being and as a species leave behind some measure of our genes into future generations. We are subject to the rules of natural selection and remain individual animals of a common species; we are only special because we designate ourselves as such.

Of more interest is how we got this way. Our fossil record shows that humans began as small apes that could only be distinguished from other apes because they moved about on two legs. The other kinds of apes at that time spent most of their day in the trees utilizing their arms as well as their legs to get about. But about 4 million years ago, the human line of ancestors apparently moved out of the trees and into the undergrowth, moving around on two legs to explore for food between patches of woods.[5] No one knows what exactly triggered this drive to upright walking, called bipedalism, but presumably it was the most efficient way to get around the habitat, so it gained those small apes some sort of feeding advantage.[6] We remained small bipedal apes for several million years, and then something happened about 1.5 million years ago. One type of those upright walking apes had a bigger brain than others, and that trait was rapidly (rapidly in evolutionary time) selected over many generations. Big brains and bipedal walking are the two physical characteristics that set humans apart from other apes.

Human brain size relative to body size is bigger than any creature on Earth. And it's not just sheer size. Our brains are a convoluted mass of tissue, electrical impulses and neuron connections that fire constantly. In some way that neuroscientists still do not exactly understand, this tissue translates into mind (that is, thought, feeling, reasoning, and consciousness). As a result, we are flexible in our responses to outside input and we change our reactions over time to any particular input because of experience. In other words, we learn. In fact, learning from experience is one of our trademarks. Unlike most other animals that are born reactive to outside stimuli, humans must *learn* how to operate in the world. Although humans are born with big brains, they are born neurologically unfinished;[7] it is only with brain growth after birth, life experience, and direct teaching that we can eventually interact in a reasonable way with the world on our own.

Like other primates, we are social creatures. But humans have the most complex network of social interactions of any animal. We rely on social interaction and social communication for just about everything; from close family to the power of the state, each human is connected to an intricate web of other humans. Social connections appear to be so important to humans that some anthropologists have suggested that the large and complex human brain evolved to keep track of all these social machinations.[8] But even with a brain that does well in keeping track of the ins and outs of social interaction, we still have to learn how to read others and how specifically to interact with them. Again, it is our large brain, combined with life experience, that teaches us how to operate as social humans.

As a result, we have developed this thing called "culture," which is a major special trait of humans. Although other animals, such as chimpanzees, have a rudimentary form of culture[9] (that is, they make tools and show variation in many patterns of behavior across groups), only humans rely on culture to live. What exactly is culture? You could ask fifty anthropologists what they mean by culture and you would surely get fifty different detailed answers. All of them, however, refer to culture more broadly than the common idea that "culture" refers to art, dance, and music. Anthropologists use the term "culture" to include not only the higher arts but also the more general use of symbols in an abstract way, the ability to make artifacts that interface with the environment, and the explosion of life beyond merely finding food and staying alive. Culture also refers to groups that have common goals and agendas that distinguish them from other groups.

In this sense, being a cultural species means we have produced a million different ways to deal with life. We are a cultural species with a million different cultures. To be a full member of a culture, an individual has to learn the ways of that particular culture to become a functioning citizen. In other words, being human means taking time learning to be human in a particular culture.

And so special parts of being human—our big brain and learning ability, our highly social way of life, our culture—all involve experience and learning. Interestingly, childhood also happens to be at the heart of that learning process.

Making Childhood

Childhood is the time of extensive brain growth during which kids learn, through play and teaching, how to manipulate objects, how to socialize with others, and begin to master the rules of culture.[10] It makes sense that stretching out this age period, from, say, ages two to seven, would be an advantage in our species to accommodate all this learning.

It would be easy to create such a life cycle stage from the life path of any mammal or primate—simply take the time before sexual maturity and stretch it out to include a long period of learning early on. This could be accomplished by either slowing down the whole path of growth, or slowing down the rates of growth and development at various ages. Either way, the early life cycle stages would be extended, sort of like stretching taffy, to the point where you can see the stages breaking into a greater number of individual segments.[11]

Most biologists believe this is precisely how human childhood was created. The scenario goes like this: Humans needed to learn so much about culture, including tool use and language and symbolism. Those individuals who stretched out the early years, spending more time learning tool use, language, symbolism, and other skills that helped them survive, obviously gained an advantage. They lived longer and had more children and passed along more genes. Unfortunately, this nice neat scenario doesn't really fit the reality of human childhood, or the way that evolution works.

Anthropologist Barry Bogin of the University of Michigan, a tall lean man with an intense gaze, believes childhood is not the result of slowing rates of growth after infancy, delaying the jump to adolescence. It just doesn't make sense, he claims. First of all, the body doesn't grow in an even way. Various human growth curves that chart the rates and timing of growth separately for the brain, body size, and the sexual organs are so complex that simply stretching out the time between infancy and adolescence won't do. Bogin believes that something much more novel took place. Childhood, he claims in a radical new theory, was *inserted* into the life cycle as an entirely new stage of life.

In Bogin's scheme, this insertion came about not to allow time for learning but because it was reproductively advantageous for parents. Children, while still dependent for food and protection and unable yet to function on their own, are independent enough that they can be cared for by others, including older children. Parents, under this scheme, can take advantage of passing along much of the responsibility of caring for younger children, allowing the parents to reproduce again. In other words, childhood evolved to increase the reproductive success of parents, allowing them to have more children, rather than to enable children more time to learn. To be sure, learning is *the* primary function of childhood, but our need to learn doesn't necessarily explain what originally gave us childhood. After all, parents have more control over what happens to children than what they themselves decide to do. It makes more sense, then, to figure out this puzzle from the perspective of the parents' reproductive success.

Bogin supports his theory with the fact that human growth curves are anything but simple. For example, the brain grows rapidly after birth and doesn't level off until about age seven. Overall, the body grows by a combination of steady growth that is interspersed with accelerated spurts, especially around age five and then right before adolescence. Teeth, which take a major caloric expenditure to grow and are vital for nutritional independence, emerge during the first year of life, then they fall out and are replaced by adult teeth between ages five and ten. And reproductive organs lie relatively dormant until about ten years of age. In other words, our childhood patterns of growth are a mosaic that both helps and hinders what children can do, and those patterns are not very coordinated. As Bogin puts it, we take just under two decades to reach full adulthood, and the physiological path to adulthood is more "sinuous" than developmentally straight.[12]

We are also a reproductively "frugal" species, Bogin notes. While the insects dole out hundreds of larvae, and fish spawn hundreds of eggs, and rodents have frequent and sizable litters, we humans usually have one infant at a time, spacing them a year or more apart. In this, we continue the primate tradition; monkeys and apes also have only one infant at a time with relatively long spaces in between.

In other words, we are a long-lived, developmentally complex, slow to mature, low-reproducing species. If the point is to have many offspring and bring them quickly to sexual maturity, how could this complex of strategies possibly be successful?

The answer, Bogin believes, lies in the ability of humans to adapt to certain features of human evolution, especially the neurological and physical dependence of infants, and incorporate that dependence into a successful reproductive strategy. Compared to primates and other mammals, humans turn out to have a relatively short period of real infancy. Phyllis Lee collected information on when food is initially introduced to youngsters in eighty-eight species of large-bodied mammals and then compared those data to cross-cultural information on humans.[13] For most mammals, babies move to solid food when they are about twice their birth weight, but they are not fully weaned until they are three to four times their birth weight. Primates push that transition even further. Weaning among primate species occurs on average when infants are over four times their birth weight, and in the apes, such as chimpanzees and orangutans, infants are at least six times their birth weight before they are on solid food all the time. But oddly enough, humans do not follow this primate trend of increasing the time spent on mother's milk. One would expect human mothers would, since our infants are born the most helpless of all species and require the fastest brain growth. Mother's milk should be needed for a very long time, at *least* as long as ape mothers provide it. But oddly enough, the opposite is true; humans more closely follow small mammals in their patterns of breast-feeding to a particular birth weight—and nothing like other primates or apes. In many cultures, babies are breast-fed until they are several years old. But mothers in these cultures also always supplement breast milk with solid foods very quickly during the first year.[14] And in industrialized nations, where breast-feeding is less common and last on average for only four months,[15] solid food is traditionally introduced when babies are about twice their birth weight, at four months or so.[16] In other words, humans are very unprimatelike, in terms of birth weight, when they introduce solid foods.

Bogin suggests that when babies are put on solid food, and then fully weaned, the intense period of maternal dependence is really over. Once a baby is off the breast, it still requires feeding, but now anyone, rather than just the mother, can do it. After weaning, kids need specialized nonadult food that can be easily digested, and even when they can handle some of the feeding process themselves, young children still need food that they can pick up and chew. But again, the key is that others, not just the mother, can provide these foods. As such, human infants move very quickly, compared to other primates, from nursing infancy to childhood—the stage where they are less dependent and anyone can provide the right foods and care.

And this is Bogin's point. Since the human pattern of growth, especially brain growth, dictates a long period from infancy to adolescence, parents must take care of kids for a long time, because they can't take care of themselves. Anthropologist Jane Lancaster says that humans are the only species that still feeds their juveniles.[17] But what is different about humans is that relatively quickly, there are options for feeding beyond what mother provides. And that is an enormous advantage from a purely evolutionary view. When women breast-feed intensely, they stop ovulating; this means a woman nursing children until they were juveniles— the stage at which other species are fully weaned—would not be fertile until her children were seven to ten years old. More important from an evolutionary perspective, if women were only fertile every ten or so years, humans would be the slowest-reproducing species on Earth—and presumably not successful at all. When confronted with a highly dependent offspring that will need care for years, it makes more sense, evolutionarily speaking, to move rapidly to weaning foods and get help with feeding from others, such as the father, family, and other group members, so that the women can conceive again.

Comparative data on the interval between births of apes and

current humans seem to support Bogin's ideas. In 1994, anthropologist Anne Zeller compared the interbirth interval (that is, the time between births) of apes and humans to figure out what makes human reproduction special.[18] In apes, births typically take place five years apart. But Zeller found that humans have much shorter interbirth intervals. In populations where nursing is the only factor delaying conception, women typically have babies three to four years apart. Over a long life span, they have many more children than do any of the apes. Humans, as Bogin's theory suggests, have decreased the interbirth interval compared with their ape cousins. As a result, they have the potential to raise a higher total number of offspring over a lifetime and are therefore evolutionarily more successful than apes. Presumably, our ancestors evolved down this path of reproductive success long ago, and that may be one reason the apes have not been particularly successful, while the human population continues to expand.

Under this scheme, childhood is an evolutionary advantageous stage of growth inserted into the human life cycle which allows kids to be nutritionally dependent but off the mother's milk, so that the mother can reproduce again. To be sure, lots of learning and development take place during childhood, but it may be that this stage did not appear in the human life cycle simply to accommodate the demands of human brain growth—which, in fact, completes its major growth at age seven—but to create a stage that allows parents to accommodate several offspring at different stages of development, with some more dependent than others. Childhood may, in fact, be part of a human assembly line of reproduction: Have a baby, wean it, and push it nutritionally into childhood, get some outside help, and then have another baby.

Ancestral Burdens?

But how exactly do humans shift the care of kids to someone else, and who exactly take up the slack?

Anne Zeller, who charted the amount of work young children do in households across the globe (see Chapter One), believes that kids themselves are very much responsible for assisting this evolutionary trajectory. As we saw in the last chapter, children in other cultures are major contributors to the economy of the household. Once weaned and once mobile, kids in other cultures do most of the child care, run errands, tend livestock, and work in the fields. And they not only bring in food for themselves, they often feed others with food gathered from the landscape. In doing so, kids in other cultures free up time for adults.[19]

The contributions by children could well have been a major factor in evolutionary terms in allowing mothers to produce more children. In support of this, Zeller found that in areas where weaning foods were not very nutritious and hard to come by, weaning was delayed. And in such circumstances, when food in general could not be gathered or made by children, the rate of overall fertility was comparatively low, and the interbirth interval stretched to five or so years. When kids can feed themselves, however, the birthrate is higher and babies are born closer together. And when children can feed themselves, applying the moniker "dependent" to them is not quite accurate.

Projecting these data back in time, Zeller suggests that a suite of human characteristics made it possible for children past weaning to contribute to subsistence. For example, at some point in our evolution, early humans began to gather, rather than just forage for food, and eventually campsites and social living evolved. Children in these systems could presumably gather for themselves, especially when appropriate foods were close at hand, such as berries and nuts. They could also hang around camp under the care of other adults. Once carrying implements were invented, children could utilize these as well. And the development of language would only have facilitated mothers giving directions to children, instructing them about food. Dependent children quickly then become less dependent.

In ancestral groups of hunters and gatherers, relatives and close friends in the band would have contributed to child care as well, allowing humans to reproduce more quickly in spite of existing offspring. Kristen Hawkes of the University of Utah has gathered information on the Hadza people of northern Tanzania, charting what happens to women with dependent children when life revolves around gathering enough to eat. Contrary to previous theories that fathers must help in caring for children—thus creating the nuclear family—Hawkes and her colleagues discovered that Hadza grandmothers fill in the gaps. These postreproductive women gathered more food than any members of the group and typically contributed their food to daughters who were nursing, or other female relatives who needed help.[20] And while children in these small groups may be a burden, they are a burden that is shared, or shifted to the older generation, allowing mothers to conceive more quickly than if they had to provide all on their own.

Bogin's schemes, Zeller's survey, and Hawkes's data combine to present an adaptive picture of ancestral human childhood. This perspective helps to explain the evolutionary purpose of childhood, rather than how it is utilized today. Parents have been biologically designed to pass on genes efficiently within the constraints of the dependent human child. They do this by reproducing at a relatively fast rate for a species of our size and longevity, especially for a species that produces such highly dependent offspring. As a response to the dependent nature of human infants, our species may have been designed to allow dependent children to be cared for, in part, by older children, grandmothers, and other family members.[21] In other words, our species devised flexible behavioral solutions to biological problems.

This scenario does not discount the tremendous amount of growth and learning that goes on during childhood. Regardless of whether childhood was inserted into the human life cycle to help parents reproduce more babies, or stretched out of the existing life cycle to allow more time for learning, it is clear that childhood is a special time, a necessary time, and a critical time for the individual human.

When Did Childhood Evolve?

When exactly did childhood first evolve? The answer lies in examination of both the fossil record and in looking at our closest relatives, the apes.

Comparing apes to humans is a reasonable method for asking questions about human development, because we are genetically very close. About 5 or so million years ago, humans and apes shared a common ancestor. At that point, our hominid ancestor and the other apes split, and each began an evolutionary journey of its own. Today there are four kinds of apes—gorillas, gibbons, orangutans, and chimpanzees, and only one kind of human, although our evolutionary tree sprouted any number of species until about thirty-five thousand years ago. We are genetically closest to the present-day chimpanzee, although there are great differences. Still, those small-brained apes are useful as benchmarks to figure out what might have happened to humans over evolutionary time.

Physiologist R. D. Martin has done just that by comparing ape and human brains, since brain size is the defining and limiting factor of humanness and surely must be implicated in the appearance of childhood.[22] Martin has discovered that in apes, brain growth is rapid before birth and relatively slower after birth. In comparison, human brain growth is rapid both before *and* after birth. This push for continuous brain growth before and after birth in humans is necessary because the infant head can only be so big to fit through the narrow bipedal pelvis. If human babies were born with head size relative to adult size that paralleled the apes, they could never fit through the birth canal. Natural selection could have opted to make the pelvic opening larger, but given the architecture of the type of pelvis needed for bipedal walking, this was impossible; with a wider pelvis, women would be unable to walk efficiently. And so natural selection opted for the other possibility—babies are born "too soon" with small heads and neurologically unfinished brains. Measured by our brain tissue, we are simply born too early.[23] But we make up for this by more than tripling our brain size from birth to age seven.[24]

The point is that sometime in our human past, we moved from a chimplike pattern of brain growth to a human pattern. That particular point is likely when childhood first appeared. But when exactly did this happen?

We know from fossil evidence and footprints that our ancestors were walking upright at least 4 million years ago. The architecture of the pelvis changed about this time from a chimp pattern of a long and narrow pelvis with a wide and unrestricted birth canal, to a more squat pelvis with a more restricted birth canal. Birth, however, would not have been a problem, because our ancestors at that time still had brains the size of a chimpanzee, about 400 cubic centimeters.[25] Their babies must have had baby chimplike brains. Then about 1.5 million years ago, at the stage called *Homo habilis,* brain size doubled, from the chimplike 400 cubic centimeters to 800 centimeters or so. At this point, the shape of the pelvic opening became a liability, and human babies had to be born with relatively smaller heads. It may be that this is the point where childhood was inserted.[26] It is a point when the human life cycle took a dramatic turn, the point where brain size became the force compelling the path of human evolution, the point where having more time for brain growth and learning was a must.

This idea is confirmed by a skeleton of a young boy that dates to 1 million years ago at the next stage of human evolution, called *Homo erectus.* This boy, discovered by Kamoya Kimeu and described by Alan Walker of Johns Hopkins University, is estimated to have had an infant head size of about 231 cubic centimeters, a relatively small brain that would have needed to grow rapidly over the next several years to reach adult size. And it must have grown during a period beyond infancy but before adolescence, when this boy perished and became a fossil. By 1 million years ago, then, humans had surely established a life cycle pattern that included a long childhood.

Childhood is a crucial time marked by physical and cognitive growth, a time when young humans learn what it means to be human. It is a time when the human body and brain develop at a rapid pace. As any parent will tell you, kids seem to grow before your eyes. But the pattern, scale, and rate of growth is not a given. Forces such as nutrition and cultural tradition can have a profound effect on the growth and development of kids, as we will see in the next chapter.

CHAPTER THREE

Growing Up

There is one sure way to make me cry. Go into my basement and head for the big plastic tubs full of winter clothes, blankets and such, and find the one marked with my daughter's name. Rummage inside, push aside the photographs, books, and toys that I am saving for her and pull out the booties she wore the first few weeks of her life, the smallest footwear in this collection. I know them well—white with pink flowers, about an inch long, and they match a one-piece baby coverall. Place those booties into my hand and you'll see the tears well up. And if you really want me to cry, pull out the rest of the footwear stashed in that tub and set them up on my desk, from smallest to most recent; the tiny blue sneakers she wore when she first started walking, and then the snow boots for her second winter; the black party shoes for her second holiday season and the white Easter shoes with the tulips that are yet another size bigger.

Line them up by size and I'll cry uncontrollably.

One of the greatest joys in life is seeing a child grow. It's also a daily tragedy, as any parent knows, because no matter how much we love this or that stage, kids just keep on growing into adults. A record of their growth in shoes or on a chart is one of the most sentimental records many parents can have. You can read in those records the day-to-day life of a child, the progress of biological growth, as well as the development of a person. And if you have been intimately involved in this process with one or more children, it is one of life's greatest experiences—and one of its greatest mysteries.

Growing is what kids do. They grow in body size, shape, and weight. Their internal organs grow. Their brains not only grow in mass but also change in organization. In fact, it is impossible to understand childhood without some understanding of growth— why and how it occurs, and what forces influence the direction of growth.

What Does It Mean to Grow?

Growth is a property of life. One reason we know a rock is not alive is because it doesn't grow. Organic matter, that is matter that is alive, grows; it not only gets larger or smaller in size but also changes composition.[1] The body and the organs which make up the body grow larger, either because the absolute number of cells increases, the volume of each cell gets larger, or the material in between cells increases.[2] Tissues, such as muscle, bone, skin, and brain, grow at different rates; they also start and stop growth at different times. For example, nerve cells that make up the central nervous system stop dividing at about eighteen weeks of gestation, but the limb bones continue growing through puberty. And skin and blood cells continue to grow throughout life. The progress of growth over the life course also varies for each tissue. In general, there are four main growth phases: the early embryo, which grows by cell division and then by differentiating those cells into body parts; childhood, in which growth focuses on maturing those systems; maturity, during which growth maintains the body and offsets wear and tear; and then the end of growth during old age when cells and organs work less well.[3]

Within the body, each tissue also has a life course. Cells which make up fat tissue, for example, increase in number before puberty, but they don't increase in size until after sexual maturity. Muscle tissue sometimes grows in that way, as well—there are cells in reserve that can mature to full capacity, even later in life. Bone growth is a special case, and the tale of bone is important, because most evaluations of childhood growth are made on stature— the growth of the skeleton, which is made up of bone tissue. In fact, more is known about the process of bone growth than any other tissue.

Early in fetal life, centers of bone growth, called centers of ossification, appear in the middle of shafts or plates of cartilage destined to become the skeleton. Slowly, the cartilage at these points is replaced by real bone tissue. None of the bones of the skeleton are fixed at birth—all of them continue to grow for decades.[4] The plates of the skull do not fully fuse until adulthood, for example. Limb bones (that is, arms and legs) are of special interest because they determine height. Unlike most other parts of the skeleton, in which ossification starts at the center and is laid down across a plate, limb bones grow from the tips, not the center. At each end of a long bone are areas of growth that remain flexible. Called epiphyses, these caps rest on the tips of long bones and allow bone cells to be deposited in layers that are eventually absorbed into the bone shaft, giving it more length.[5] At adolescence, under the influence of the hormonal changes that occur at puberty, the caps or epiphyses fuse onto the bone shaft and linear growth ends—the individual has achieved his or her adult height.[6] But this does not mean that bone tissue growth stops. Bone cells continually divide and are replaced over a lifetime. Eventually, as part of the aging process, the destruction of bone tissue outpaces the replacement of tissue and bones become fragile.[7]

It is this ongoing process that makes bone tissue so flexible. During childhood, nongenetic influences, such as nutrition and disease, can affect how bones take shape and how tall a person will become. Strong as the skeleton might be, it is still highly vulnerable. As such, the skeleton is often an indicator of overall health and well-being.

Growth is also not the same for everyone. Girls and boys, for example, mature at different rates, and this is true of most animal species. The difference begins in utero and can be documented about halfway through gestation, when the female fetus is about three weeks more mature than the male fetus.[8] During childhood, boys and girls go through the same body markers of development, but girls reach each level faster. Girls, for example, cut their canine teeth almost a full year before boys. At adolescence, girls are about two years ahead of boys in their maturational process. Boys end up taller on average only because they experience more overall years of growth during adolescence.

Growth is masterminded, in essence, by hormones. These internally manufactured chemicals are designed to be received by and affect certain target tissues by receptors that are designed to attach to that chemical and react. According to growth specialist J. M. Tanner, there are at least a dozen hormones that are important for normal human growth, including cortisol, thyroxine, testosterone, estrogen, and melatonin, all originating from different organs and glands.[9] The pituitary gland, which rests at the base of the brain between the eyes, and the hypothalamus are of special importance to growth because they begin the cascade of hormonal release. Initiator hormones of the hypothalamus signal to the pituitary to release hormones, and those pituitary hormones in turn signal other organs to release their chemicals, which in turn affect target tissues.[10]

Of special interest with regard to children is human growth hormone, because it influences adult height and muscle growth. No one knows exactly how growth hormone works, only that it has an effect on long bones, and those with deficient levels of it can reach normal height when injected with a synthesized version. Less clear is whether those with a normal genetic profile for growth can have their height increased, or speeded up, with the same injections. There are a number of other growth factors (that is, other chemical agents) that are less well known but which still have a dramatic impact on the rate and end point of growth. In other words, the biological infrastructure that supports and controls changes in height, weight, shape, and maturation of the body during childhood is much more complex than one simple growth hormone.

Human Growth

Every species has a typical life history (that is, each animal follows a biologically designed course through life). There are individual variations in this course, but in general, there are species specific times of growth. As anthropologist Holly Smith puts it, "When to be born, when to be weaned, when to stop growing, when to reproduce, and when to die are basic elements of mammalian life history, and species vary in both absolute and relative timing of these events."[11] And the way a creature takes shape is intimately involved in that timing. As Smith explains, a mouse and an elephant are very different animals, and it would be a surprise if the timing of their growth and the pattern of their shape were the same. Elephant body mass, it turns out, is 27 percent skeleton, whereas the mouse body is only 4 percent skeleton. If the percentages were reversed, the elephant would fall apart and the mouse couldn't move. Elephants also have singleton births, while mice have litters, and even this reproductive event is part of a specific life history trajectory. It would make no sense for the mouse, which lives fast and dies relatively soon, to have one offspring at a time, while the elephant, which moves slowly and eats a great deal, would have no time to guard and feed for a litter of baby elephants. In other words, their lives fit together in a biologically appropriate way; they make sense.

Humans have a life history pattern similar to other primates but different from other mammals, in that we achieve sexual maturity relatively quickly, considering our growth trajectory. In fact, our skeleton has not quite reached adult size, and even our adult teeth are not all in at the time of sexual maturity. This is an anomaly. Other mammals, such as mice, grow up quickly, reproduce, and then die; but primates live a long time, and we might expect humans would begin to reproduce much later in that long life. What's the hurry to achieve sexual maturity? Long-lived and big animals, it seems, give birth to proportionally small babies—human infants, for example, must grow rapidly and for a long time before they reach adult size—and so the females of the species are equipped relatively early in the life cycle to produce those small infants.

Human growth, then, follows a pattern that makes sense for a big mammal that lives for a long time. We are born relatively small, grow rapidly and for a long time, are able to reproduce relatively early, and reach the completion of growth and maturity rather late in the life cycle.

Brain Growth

Head and brain growth are, of course, intimately connected. Before birth, human brain growth is quite rapid when compared to other mammals and other primates. At birth, in fact, the human brain is more near its adult weight than any other organ. After birth, that rate of increase of the brain and skull slows down (although it is still faster than any other animal), just as the rate of growth for other body parts is accelerating. At two years of age, a child's brain has reached 75 percent of its adult weight—which is why kids have such big heads in proportion to the rest of their bodies—and by ten years of age, the head is only 5 percent under its adult size. But it's not simply brain tissue that grows over time. Various components that make up the brain grow and mature at different rates and different times. The brain, like all of the body, is a dynamic system—throughout life the neural cells and supporting material in the brain change according to growth, experience, disease, and aging.[12]

The brain is composed of both neurons, which transmit impulses, and support cells, called neuroglia, which make up much of the volume of the brain early in life. We are born with all the neurons we will ever get, but the character of those cells and their connections change dramatically over a lifetime.[13] Each neuron is composed of a cell body, a variety of organelles or particles that seem to help in the transmission of signals, and cell protrusions that look like fingers. Some of these fingers are dendrites, filaments that receive messages from other neurons. Others are axons, filaments which carry signals away from the brain cells to other cells, sometimes in other parts of the body. A nerve cell in the brain, for example, can have an axon that reaches all the way down into the foot. Together, the dendrites and axons make up a network that can relay signals throughout the brain and all over the body.

But the network is not a neatly wired structure; gaps between axons and dendrites require special chemicals to pass signals from cell to cell, and those gaps are extremely wide in young brains. Prenatal and postnatal growth involves not so much an increase in the number of neuronal cells, as maturation of the connections among those cells, and between those cells and the rest of the body. Over time, myelin sheaths, or insulating material, is deposited around the axons, which makes for a more direct route for signals. Dendrites also continue to grow after birth, increasing and complicating the branching networks upon which impulses can travel. The signals are sent faster and more efficiently as the brain matures, because the connections are cleaner.

It takes a lot of energy to run this developing system; a two-year-old's brain uses up as much glucose as an adult's brain, and a three-year-old's brain runs at a metabolic rate over twice that of an adult.[14]

Also, that young brain is highly sensitive. Neural pathways are opened or closed depending on exposure, and the connections in general can be improved with stimulation. Like a muscle, the brain does best biologically when it is used. Pediatric neurologist Ann Barnet writes that the developing child brain operates under a "Use it or lose it" rule. Every motor movement, every intellectual event, every emotional experience that a child encounters will influence brain development. And it's not all about increases. Some circuits will become permanent, while others will be turned off. Lest parents worry, there are literally zillions of possible neural paths. But without any experience—to take an example, say, if a child is shut in a dark room and cut off from everyday life—those circuits will shut down forever.

There are also sensitive periods for some specific learning abilities. Learning a second language, for example, is easy in childhood but usually much more difficult in adulthood. Neural networks are formed, changed, eliminated, and restructured in a way that science still does not completely understand. But in general, brain growth is highly influenced by the environment for which it is designed to operate. Biology, in this case, as in all others, is intimately entwined with experience.

There are clear connections between specific parts of the brain and body movement. Babies can move their arms well before they can move their legs, and maturation of those parts of the brain which control that movement reflect this pattern of maturation. The neuronal systems that help with fine motor control, for example, are not fully mylinated until the age of four. And mylination of those parts of the brain that have to do with mind (that is, consciousness) continue into puberty. Clearly, psychological, intellectual, and physical development are both limited and enhanced by the progress of brain development over childhood and beyond.

Growth Curves

The oldest published record charting the growth of a child comes from the eighteenth century. Count Philibert Geréneau de Montbeillard kept a close and accurate record of his son from birth to eighteen years of age. The count charted his son's progress in height each year, showing a growth curve, as well as increments of growth per year, which also demonstrated the son's early childhood and adolescent growth spurts.[15]

Once children began attending school in the 1700s, they became fodder for those interested in charting growth. Several studies established what we now call standard growth curves, always with an eye to figure out what would be "normal" for a child of any particular age. By the 1800s, these curves were used not only to evaluate the health of children but also had a political agenda, since this was the time when children were entering the work force as factory laborers, and child advocates feared for their health and their lives.[16]

The emphasis on children as indicators of population health was further emphasized in the United States with the work of anthropologist Franz Boas in the late 1800s. Boas collected data on the growth of children in comparison to their European emigrant parents and clearly demonstrated that environment, in the guise of nutrition and health care, had a marked effect on how children grow and on their eventual adult height. Today we accept this notion as fact, but back then, people believed that heredity, not environment, determined everything about people. Since that time, a number of studies have shown that the children of emigrants to first world countries are on the whole taller and heavier than their parents, whether they are Japanese kids growing up in Hawaii, or Mexican and Mayan kids growing up in the United States.[17]

In any case, the growth rate of children over time and all over the world is surprisingly regular when kids receive adequate nutrition. Typically, there is a rapid rate of growth in height during the first year, a slower and more steady increase from one to about seven years of age, where another small spurt occurs, regular increases in height from age seven to right before puberty, followed by a huge adolescent growth spurt, after which the rate of increase in height slows and then stops. Children also grow seasonally; they experience more growth in the spring than the fall, and in certain climates they grow more during the dry season when food is available and the risk of illness low rather than the wet season.[18] In fact, studies on the growth of children in the United States show that any child grows three times as fast in his or her fastest season than the child's slowest. In other countries with different climates, this pattern ranges according to monsoon season. In rural Nepal, for example, 71 percent of the children are underweight, 31 percent are severely stunted, and 10 percent are wasted during the monsoon season, when food is less available and diseases such as upper respiratory infections and diarrhea are rampant.[19] Seasonality, in this case, is a major influence on yearly growth and on overall lifetime patterns of growth. Children experiencing deprivation are quite good at catch-up growth if this catch-up occurs during periods when the body is physiologically primed to respond to the boost.

The Environment of Growth

Each child carries a genetic blueprint that guides his or her growth pattern. One good predictor of adult height is the height of both parents. But a prediction based on parents is, at the same time, a shaky prediction, because adult form is also molded by a life course of outside influences. In other words, size and shape are formed by an interaction of genes and environment.

Human infants, on average, are born about the same weight around the globe, and for the first six months or so, they all weigh about the same.[20] Presumably, breast-feeding provides a standard within which infants, barring famine, thrive at a standard species-specific rate.[21] But after six months, individual patterns assert themselves. Even identical twins differ in size and weight after this initial breast-fed period.

Research has shown that height, weight, specific growth rates and patterns are all subject to a variety of nongenetic factors. Nutrition, of course, plays a major role. But socioeconomic status of the family, a history of illness, and long-term psychological stress, including family trauma and war, can also have major effects on both growth patterns of the child and eventual adult size. And various environmental factors, such as altitude, urbanization, sanitation, and climate, can also have an effect.

Studies have shown that malnutrition in particular can stop cell division, but once health is restored, the cells will start dividing again if the nutrition is resumed quickly enough. Those who eat too much in early childhood have other worries. No one knows if overnutrition early in life can increase the total number of fat cells, or whether it just pumps up existing cells. This issue is important in affluent cultures—obese adults can lose material within fat cells, but they can't lose the number of fat cells they have without having them sucked out through liposuction. Without such surgery, fat cells are with us forever.

Across the board, children of families with high socioeconomic status begin childhood taller and weighing more and continue in that vein until adulthood.[22] No one is quite sure what it is about socioeconomic status that creates the difference, but clearly the combination of good nutrition, adequate health care, less exposure to infectious diseases makes for bigger children and adults. Obviously, changes in economy, lifestyle, and diet can have a dramatic effect on childhood growth. In Japan, for example, the Ministry of Education has been keeping records on child height and weight since 1900. Every spring, Japanese children have been measured in school, and those records have demonstrated a regular increase in height since the turn of the century. But suddenly, between 1960 and 1975, there was an incremental rise in height, and the usual difference between urban kids, who were taller, and rural kids suddenly disappeared.[23] Researchers traced the source of this change to the school lunch program, where milk had been introduced after World War II.

The nuances of parental style can also have a major impact on growth, even when parents believe they are doing what is best for their kids. In an extensive study of kids from birth to childhood in the Amele of lowland Papua New Guinea, Carol Jenkins and colleagues found that although Amele babies are born a bit small, they grow just fine for the first six months. But at that point, their rate of improvement falls behind until Amele kids are much smaller than one might expect. Living with the Amele, rather than just measuring them, proved the best way to figure out what was happening.[24] It seems that Amele mothers, like all mothers around the globe, begin to supplement breast-feeding with other food around ten months of age. But unlike mothers in other cultures, these supplements are not particularly nutritious—babies are traditionally given only fruit juice or soup and no solid food. The Amele believe that breast milk grows stronger and more nutritious as the child grows, and so they supplement infrequently. Jenkins believes that the drop in the rate of infant growth around this time occurs because juice and soup are simply not enough when babies are turning into toddlers.

Food, both in number of calories as well as the nutritious value of food, is, of course, essential for adequate growth. In study after study, both in the West and in other cultures, children who do not get enough to eat, or not enough protein, or not enough vitamins, grow slower and often are never able to catch up even when their diet is corrected.[25] Also, kids with inadequate nutrition not only grow slower, they also reach maturity later.[26] Not enough food, not enough good food, rampant infectious disease, and inadequate sanitation are the killers of children. And these influences are, of course, the markers of poverty into which many children throughout the world are born.

Markers of Development

Every parent wants to know that his or her child is growing normally; we are not only concerned with physical growth but with mental growth as well. Does our child do all the things that a child of this age should be doing? This concern is justified. Many problems, discovered early, can be corrected or modified. And that's why a visit to the pediatrician or family practice doctor once a year includes a checklist for the child. Can she talk? Can he hold a cup without spilling the contents? Does she negotiate the stairs? Physicians are trying to spot developmental problems, so that they can help. But these well-meaning checklists, and comparisons among various children, can also lead to trouble. When my daughter was eighteen months old, she saw a nurse practitioner for a well baby visit. The nurse asked me if she could say fifteen words and I said I had no idea. She could talk a lot, and she seemed to be perfectly normal in this regard, but quite frankly, I had never added up the number of words she used. Should I count the babble that only I and her father understood? Would half words figure into this list? The nurse fixed me with a disgruntled look and said,

"Maybe you should talk to her in more complex sentences." I burst out laughing, knowing as I do that any kind of drill is useless in this regard (see Chapter Four) and that I always spoke to my daughter in the same way that I spoke to anybody, with all the complexities. Six months later, at age two, we had a more reasonable check with the pediatrician and he asked the more relevant questions: "Can you understand her? Can she understand you?" The point is, lists can't be taken too seriously, and most pediatricians, child-care advice writers, and health care workers know this. In fact, if you peruse popular books on child development, you'll see not only a variety of checklists for charting your child's development but also a strong suggestion by authors for parents to realize these milestones come at various times and rates; every child is different. Think of these charts as guides: Be flexible, they seem to say.

Take for example the milestones in *Caring for Your Baby and Young Child*, a manual sanctioned by the American Academy of Pediatrics.[27] Each chapter describes an age: one to two, two to three, and so on. And within those chapters there are shaded boxes that list physical, emotional, cognitive, and social milestones. By the end of the second year, for example, a child should be able to walk alone, carry large toys, kick a ball, imitate others, play make-believe, and be aware of self, among other things. By the end of the third year, that child should be able to kick the ball in a straight line, make mechanical toys work, imitate others even more, have a concept of time, and play make-believe in more elaborate ways. What is interesting in these lists is that nowhere does this book tell the parent exactly when these abilities should appear—just that eventually they should be there. And some of those skills appear the previous year, such as make-believe and imitation, and are just refined through the next year. Even in chart form, as some books put these developmental milestones, various skills appear as lines that cross ages, not as pinpoints that mark a specific age. For example, in the *Children's Medical Guide* from Columbia University's College of Physicians and Surgeons, there is a chart of fifty-three skills over six years.[28] Those abilities, such as "can dress without help" or "copies housework," appear as long lines over the various months of development. Some children, they show, can dress themselves starting at three years of age, while others might start to don their own clothes two years later. In other words, the lists are guides, not checklists, and parents should see them as such.

And when we do set our mind into thinking that our child should have all these skills when we read them, we're bound to be disappointed. I remember looking at a book on infancy when my daughter was about three months old. The book tried very hard to present a reasonable list of development—your three-month-old "should" be doing this and "might" be doing that. On that list, I saw that some three-month-olds "might" be laughing and I had seen no signs of laughing. I was devastated. Was my daughter unhappy? Was it my fault, was I not entertaining her as a good parent should? After grappling with these depressing thoughts and realizing that I was being silly, I closed the book and vowed I would never open a child guide book again (a vow I didn't keep, of course). In the same way, comparing among children can also be dangerous. If, as these books point out, children come to these skills with such variability, we run the risk of being disappointed when our child is a later starter on something, or feeling superior when our child starts "early." Such labeling is not good for anyone.

It's also important to realize that many of these stages are culturally designated (that is, pertain only to children who have the particular experience of this culture). For example, when T. Barry Brazelton or Penelope Leach talk about separation anxiety and fear of strangers as normal developmental stages that we should expect from our children, with advice on how to deal with it, they are talking only about children who are separated from their parents.[29] In many cultures, children are always around their parents and immediate family, and there is no such thing as separation, so how could they have this kind of anxiety? Or think about the various sleep problems that confound parents in our culture. Leach says that a child must learn to deal with the feelings of abandonment that come with waking up alone. But if a child grows up in a culture where no one sleeps alone, this is not a normal, expected developmental stage.

Many of the charted skills in these books are tied to how Western children play. Building blocks, putting puzzles together, riding a tricycle, using crayons and paper—these are not items that most children in the world have. Although we believe that working with these toys is a sure sign of development, there are probably other signs of developmental skill that all children share, regardless of their toy chest. This cultural bias is apparent in the way development guides talk about social development. The ability to share, play nicely, or make friends with new kids all come into question when we step outside Western culture. Children who grow up in cultures where sharing is part of the very fabric of that culture will know how to share right away, or they will be quickly taught the value of sharing, because individualism is not favored as it is in the West. In fact, in some cultures, there is nothing to share because all goods, even toys, are communally owned. In the same way, children from these cultures need not learn to stand in line, sit quietly in class, or deal with strangers. In other words, many of the actions that we in America see as developmental milestones are really just culturally initiated learned behaviors that we teach our kids. They are not universal or particularly useful signs of development. We should, therefore, be cautious when forming a picture of our own child as having achieved or not achieved some stage based on charts that only refer to one set of ideas, and one culture.

As parents, we also have to realize that our own personal abilities and goals color how we view the development of our children. For example, parents who are enthusiastic readers will obviously want children who also love reading, or parents who are adept conversationalists will expect their kids to be good with words as well. My family loves to talk, and I have enjoyed watching the development of my daughter's speech patterns; I can hardly wait until we are able to chat like adults. But my partner is an artist and for him, the most exciting thing is to see her draw a circle, or something that might resemble a tree. In fact, one day after being with her all day, he turned to me, exhausted, and said, "I have never talked so much in my life." To me, a day spent talking with her all the time seems normal, although I pay little attention to her drawings and paintings. In both cases, we "expect" our daughter to have talents in these areas, ignoring the fact that she might not have the same abilities or interests that we do. And so our expectations for our children are influenced, even mandated, by not just culture, but by our own abilities, goals, and experience. Simply acknowledging these prejudices, and thinking about *why* some developmental stage is important, can be liberating. In doing so, we loosen our expectations and let our children off the hook.

Kids grow in other ways, as well as physically. They somehow mature into social beings, become part of a family and a community, and eventually they become independent and no longer need our care. But to accomplish this, children have to figure out how to understand the world in all its complexity and how to interact with others. In the next chapter, I'll look at how they communicate with the world—through language—and how that language also influences how they see the world.

CHAPTER FOUR

Kidspeak

From the time a baby first begins to talk, a whole new world opens up, both for the baby and for his or her caretakers. From this point on, communication will be a mutual dance of speaking and listening. He or she will start to combine those bits of words into intelligible sentences. Like the rest of us, she will try to adhere to the rules of acceptable grammar, but even within those rules she will create an infinite number of word combinations. Someday she might become a writer, a teacher, or an actress and make a living by words. And everyone will forget those days when the baby had nothing to say.

Talking is a unique ability of the human species. And yet we are not born chatting a blue streak. Rather, we *acquire* language. We have a particular biological predisposition to speak and various physiological adaptations that allow us to communicate through language. But it takes years to actually figure out how to use all that equipment.

Language is one of those human arenas in which biology intersects with culture. We may be hard-wired to speak, but how we speak and what we say is grounded in who we are and what we have experienced. The journey of language acquisition, including the cultural influences, occurs early in life. Learning to speak, learning to communicate through language, learning to use language to get by, is *the* major preoccupation of kids. The larger question is why we have this ability in the first place.

Is Human Talk Unique?

Early on, our ancestors probably communicated as most other primates do (that is, in rather sophisticated ways). Extensive work on other primates shows that these animals, our close relatives, not only produce acoustically complex sounds but their noises also carry specific and important information.[1] They mark their territory with calls and keep mating competitors out.[2] Monkeys warn each other about predators and sometimes signal if the predator is coming from the sky or the ground.[3] The scream of a young monkey can tell its mother if there is a real threat or if he is just playing, just like the quality of the yell of a baby tells its mother if danger is near or he's just unhappy.[4]

But these animals do not use vocalizations to the degree that humans do. Ape language projects that have been conducted have made this abundantly clear. In the 1950s, two households attempted to teach apes to speak. Thinking that instruction and practice would prove or disprove their ability to speak, researchers brought baby chimpanzees into their homes and treated them like their own children. Over time, the chimps picked up a few intelligible words and made a mess of the house—and that was it. Apes, scientists finally figured out, don't have the vocal anatomy to speak and there is no use in trying to get them to do so. In the 1960s, another group of scientists worked with a chimpanzee named Washoe to teach her American Sign Language (ASL), a system of gestures, not words, that has the properties of human language. Washoe proceeded to learn to use about 100 signs, mostly food requests.[5] Washoe also lied and made jokes in ASL, indicating a certain social panache. Critics felt that Washoe was simply imitating her teachers and that her use of ASL was a testimony to the mimicking power of chimpanzees. It might have given some indication of her intelligence, but it did not mean chimps had real linguistic capabilities. Washoe couldn't make sentences longer than two signs, for example, and she had no syntax.[6] Other chimpanzees have learned to move plastic symbols around on a board and make some sense with these "words," and some can operate a console with various symbols. But again, their performance only demonstrates that they can take instruction and mimic, that they understand that certain symbols stand for certain objects, and they can make their food wishes known. But is this real communication through language?

And then along came Kanzi, a bonobo chimpanzee who is today's new linguistic star. What makes Kanzi so amazing is not just that he's the best chimp so far in terms of language but that initially he wasn't formally taught about language—he simply picked it up on his own. Kanzi was raised by a chimpanzee foster mother, Matata, who never really comprehended what the language experiments were all about. But when anthropologist Sue Savage-Rumbaugh and her colleagues turned to Kanzi, they discovered that he had already learned to communicate just by being with Matata during her training. He could easily use the symbol board and communicate about what those symbols represented. Researchers soon discovered that Kanzi was capable of much more. He can hear words and translate them into visual symbols. He seems to have some comprehension of syntax, although he can't produce it himself. Most startling, Kanzi understands spoken English. He responds appropriately to spoken directions, such as "Put the soap on the apple," the first time he hears them. And the fact that he does this without instruction suggests that the human ability to order language might be shared by chimpanzees, or one species of chimpanzee, or maybe just one chimp. It may also be that Kanzi is so good at the rudiments of language because he learned it so young, like a small child; and there may be critical periods for language in chimpanzees as there are in human kids.[7] In any case, Kanzi explodes the myths that the human ability for language is ours alone. At the very least, his behavior suggests that our language ability has very old and deep roots.

The Biology of Talking and Listening

What makes human speech different is that we are able to produce a range of noises with great subtly, and we have the cognitive ability to both hear and interpret these sounds. We are also able to combine basic meaningless units of sounds, called phonemes, into meaningful words which we then combine into sentences. The progress of this kind of communication actually flows along two tracks. Kids not only have to talk, they also have to listen and understand. For some less verbal kids, they know exactly what is being said, even when they don't say much themselves. Ask any one-year-old where his or her eyes or ears are and he or she will be happy to point to the appropriate body parts. In fact, pediatricians use the pointing of body parts as a cognitive developmental marker—to understand "foot," even if you can't say the word "foot," is to reassure everyone that the brain is developing normally, even if the child hasn't yet mastered making the appropriate sounds.

Speech begins with forcing air out of the lungs; the rib cage contracts and air is exhaled from the lungs into the windpipe and out the mouth and nose. Sound can also be made while inhaling air, but speech occurs as air flows out. For all animals, air passes through the larynx, an organ which rests in the neck like a gate through which air must pass. Vocal cords hang within the larynx and as air passes through these flaps of tissue they vibrate. Speech is an anatomically different form of vocalization because of the position of the larynx. In other animals, the larynx lies high in the neck very close to the back of the tongue; most of the air is expelled through the nose and most of the sounds that nonhuman primates make are nasal. In humans, however, the larynx has migrated down, allowing passage of air through the mouth as well.[8] The relatively small and mobile human tongue can push the air up, back, and around, making the mouth a resonating chamber that produces a variety of phonemes or bits of sound that then make up words. These mouth acrobatics include the regular vowels and consonants, as well as clicks and pops. Add to this the ability to control the passage of air for intonation and emphasis, lips that can stop and start the passage of air with a certain flair, and you have the myriad ways that people talk. But there is a risk to these vocal acrobatics. The larynx is now so far down in the windpipe that food that would normally pass right into the stomach has more room to plug the airway. Human babies, more than any other animal, are at risk for choking.

Interestingly, babies are born with their larynx higher up, more like other animals; this allows them to both breast-feed and breathe with ease. But with development, the larynx moves down. This is one reason the utterances of little kids are so mushy—they don't yet have the vocal anatomy to make accurate sound production.

We hear words because our ears are designed to pick up vibrations in the air. In terms of hearing language, impulses from sound are transmitted through the brain in a complex and twisted way. The first gateway is the thalamus, called the "busiest control center of the brain,"[9] which lies deep within the brain. Intersecting with autonomic systems, this is where the body will get the message to react, without apparent thought, to sudden noises. When we scream in fright or laugh out loud, the reaction occurs at this subcortical level. From there, communication becomes a cortical process.[10] Impulses are sent to the primary auditory cortex, two sections of tissue on either side of the head behind each ear. Like so many sensory inputs that cross from one side of the brain to the other, sound entering the left ear is sent to the primary auditory cortex behind the right ear, and vice versa. Within this part of the cortex, sound is "mapped" (that is, analyzed for loudness, location, and whether the mind should even pay attention). In a sense, this primary auditory cortex is a filter that orders all the incoming noises and makes initial sense of what we hear. From there, information is sent to an area called Wernicke's area, which rests close to the left ear and is the region responsible for integrating the sounds of speech with all the other information received at the same time, such as sight and touch. In fact, humans are left-brain dominant for language. But this laterization is not fixed. Children who experience brain damage to the left side can develop excellent skills because the right side of the brain will compensate over time.[11] In that sense, the brain is plastic, especially during the early years of growth.

The production of speech relies on other parts of the brain. Studies of stroke victims have identified a region high up on the left side of the brain, known as Broca's area, that has some role in guiding speech production.[12] Research has also shown that there is so much variation in these areas, and so much variation in how stroke victims react, that it's far more complex than simply drawing a line and outlining some simple area of speech production.[13]

It's also important to realize that nothing in the brain operates as simply as the above description might imply. Speech comprehension and production, like most things the brain does, involve other areas of the brain, as well. Also, when we listen to someone talking, there are all sorts of other pieces of information that become part of our comprehension at that moment—what we see, our memories of that person or other events, concentration, distraction, feeling a gas pain—we handle so many mental tasks at once that isolating the road map of speech is definitely impossible.

All animals, including humans, are constantly living in a hub-bub of sensory information, and yet we are able to concentrate on certain parts and ignore others. As yet, no one knows exactly how the brain does this. Recent technological advances in brain imaging, especially the use of MRI (magnetic resonance imaging), is just now allowing scientists to watch the brain in operation as it processes verbal information. (When brain cells are activated, they use more oxygen, and so blood flows to that particular brain tissue, which can be followed on the MRI.) The MRI is noninvasive. Just by having the subject sit still for a while (which admittedly is difficult for small children), the machine can pass over the head and pick up on blood flow and demonstrate a change from a less active state to a more active state. These pictures of brain activity produce a visual map and indicate which parts of the brain respond when hearing language or which parts attend when producing language. For example, researchers have shown that people who learn two languages simultaneously as children process those languages differently than adults who pick up a second language later in life.[14]

The human ear seems to be specially adapted to picking up on the quickly changing frequencies of consonants and vowels.[15] Being able to hear is necessary for good articulation of language. Deaf children can learn to talk, but their speech production is hampered because they have never heard the words. But deaf children have no trouble understanding sign language or reading lips. Their auditory mechanisms might be damaged, but their brains are clearly ready to talk.

Although it may seem that the basics of speech production—the ability to hear and comprehend language—has been all figured out, nothing could be further from the truth. We know that sound is taken in by the ear, that it is passed along to areas of the brain for analysis, and that sometimes the body reacts. And we know that a person can make words and form sentences and that it takes some years past infancy for this to happen. But so much of this process is still a mystery. All we can say for certain is that the ability to communicate by spoken language is a biological feature of human beings. It is hard-wired into ourselves as surely as other physical abilities, such as walking on two legs.

Why Do We Talk?

Language is complex because it not only originates with an individual, it also involves one or more receivers. Use of language includes speech production, hearing, receiving sounds, and then making sense of all this. Therefore, the evolution of language must have included all these systems, including the overriding fact that language is communication. But why do humans communicate primarily in this fashion?

Some believe that language is key to understanding human nature, that the urge to communicate by speaking is the reason we have big brains. Because Kanzi the bonobo understands syntax, the common ancestor of chimpanzees and humans, which lived about 5 million years ago, may have had the basic wiring for language, and when humans separated from this common ancestor, they presumably exploited this baseline ability. Areas of the brain now devoted to speech production and understanding were probably co-opted away from other communicative neural systems and cobbled together for this special ability. In that sense, language may have evolved part way in a piggyback fashion to other human mental abilities.[16]

But why this push toward the verbal channel? One possibility is the combination of our social selves and our material culture. William Calvin, a neuroscientist, and Derek Bickerson, a linguist, contend that language is an excellent way of refining interpersonal interactions in a society that functions almost primarily through social relationships.[17] Along with language, humans have a fine sense of who has done what to whom and why this matters. These social rules are much like the rules of syntax, and so the deep structures of language, Calvin and Bickerson suggest, have probably been selected as part of our social heritage.

But the final push for language in humans, they believe, came when brain size expanded, because of compelling reasons to make better and better tools. For millions of years, hominids used stone tools to butcher meat. But about half a million years ago, our toolbox became much more complex—awls for sewing clothes, finely fashioned spear points, and thin honed scraping tools. Making and using tools like these is not a simple matter. One has to be confronted with a problem, imagine how something besides hands, feet, and teeth could help with this problem, know that some natural material, such as stone or wood, could be fashioned into something else, and then make the tool. Tool use also implies communication between individuals and maybe even communication across generations. Tool use, then, is a social phenomenon, not just a technological one, and it's hard to imagine an assemblage of complex tools without thinking of speech as an integral part of that phenomenon. But the scenario Calvin and Bickerson suggest doesn't hold up when observing current-day hunters and gatherers who use the type of tools that our ancestors might have used.[18] In fact, only a few people make new tools; the rest learn to use them by quiet observation. In other words, the engineering and design of tools and technology is not particularly important to language, but the social situation in which they are developed and used might be.

It's more likely that language became important because of its social advantage. Leslie Aiello and Robin Dunbar, examining the fossil record, have compared the group size of our ancestors with the current group size in other primates. As a result, they have suggested that at some point, talking took the place of social grooming.[19] According to their theory, natural selection favored the drive to talk because group size had gotten too big for grooming alone to work as a social glue and verbalizing was the only way our ancestors could keep together. Anthropologist Robbins Burling agrees and claims that having linguistic skill is an advantage in all societies. Language can be instrumental in getting you a mate or helpful in achieving high social status. In other words, those who speak better pass on more genes to the next generation, and so talking is favored by natural selection.[20] Language is here in its elaborate form because it serves a social purpose.[21] We are a talking species because we are a highly interactive species.

Like all anatomical changes, the move to language must have been relatively gradual and may have gone through various stages like any anatomical or behavioral system.[22] We know that chimps have some of the mental ability necessary to use language, and smaller-brained primates have the ability to communicate complex information. Recently, scientists have also found a homologue to Wernicke's area in the brains of chimpanzees.[23] As such, language, no matter its magnificent versatility, is just another step further along this continuum.

Acquiring Language

Other animals might communicate, and often in very sophisticated ways, but only humans pronounce words, make up sentences, describe what is not at hand, convey meaning about the past and future, and have a running internal dialogue with themselves. As anthropologist Lee Cronk says, "Language deserves some special attention because it is, after all, the medium of so much cultural transmission and so many of our efforts at manipulation and persuasion."[24]

More remarkable is the fact that this path, from guttural noises to sophisticated communication, is so much a part of the basic human hard-wiring. In the 1950s, linguists believed that human speech was learned. They felt that children hear talking from others and therefore simply pick up on vocabulary and syntax, the rules of word order, by listening to others. But linguist Noam Chomsky changed our ideas about all that. Chomsky made a convincing argument for a biological basis for language. He felt that the ability to talk, the ability to take in words and make sense of them, was part of the human blueprint.[25] The rules of language, according to his view, were part of a deep structure that is innate in every child and that no other animal shares this ability. Chomsky's view is often called the "innatist" approach. It was, of course, in sharp contrast to the ideas of B. F. Skinner and others, who at the time believed that only through verbal stimuli from adults and repeated practice will kids learn to talk.[26] This debate, which still goes on today within linguistic circles, is part of a larger debate about how much biology (nature) and how much learning and experience (nurture) bring to the expression of *any* human behavior. These days the nature part is gaining new understanding—and new allies—simply because of advancements in biological knowledge. Work on the role of genes, how the brain works, and the details of how various body systems really function has placed the focus on nature. But any reasonable scientist would agree that everything humans and all animals do is always a mix of both nature and nurture. And the capacity for language is one of the best examples of that mix.

Even though language takes many forms, and there is great diversity of expression among the languages of the world, communicating through language is one of the basic facts of human nature. There may not be specific "language genes" or a "language organ" per se, but hearing words, making sense of those words as well as producing chat, is part of our humanness.[27]

Since Chomsky's time, others have tested this idea and confirmed that children do innately know how to talk. They have a predisposition to order sound syntactically (that is, in a way that will make sense to the listener), even with no exposure to the rules of a particular language. In fact, talking is one of the few things that is so hard-wired that while there might be variation in the timing of the acquisition of language, everyone eventually talks. There is only one very rare genetic disease in which those afflicted might know how to talk, but their syntax is scrambled and they really can't communicate. Brain damage too can alter the ability to produce speech or understand what is spoken. But more remarkable is the *consistency* with which people talk. No matter the culture, no matter the intelligence of the individual, people all talk.[28] In that sense, language is one of the major species-specific abilities that we have. Just like being compelled to stand on two legs and walk, children are compelled to talk.[29] And they don't need to be *taught* how to form words or how to construct grammatically correct sentences. They just do it.

Parents are especially confused about this issue because they watch little kids struggle with language for several years, and they see that some kids are verbally able more quickly than others.[30] Parenting, they figure, must make a difference in language acquisition; surely parents who talk endlessly to their kids, drill them on grammar, and read to improve their vocabulary must have the most verbally advanced children. Parents, in other words, often think they need to teach language.

They are wrong. Linguist Stephen Pinker calls this belief "folklore." No amount of talking directly to kids, no amount of verbal drilling, will make one child talk earlier or better than another. Looking at language and children across cultures, scientists have found that children use all sorts of strategies to learn language, and all these strategies work fine.[31] In fact, language acquisition seems to be a "well-buffered" ability that will develop as long as general conversation is part of the environment.[32] As Pinker puts it, "Children deserve most of the credit for the language they acquire."[33]

Pinker says this because children instinctively know things about language that no one could have taught them. The deep structure of language, as Noam Chomsky explained, is simply part of being human. For example, kids very quickly understand that words don't make sense just because they are set in a line. They realize instead that words are really grouped into meaningful phrases and that these phrases can then be moved around to alter the meaning of a sentence. They also know how to make plurals and do this with abandon when encountering new words. They know a question deserves an answer. And when they make mistakes, those mistakes actually make linguistic sense. In fact, what parents attempt to teach them is more linguistically simple than kids are wired to understand. They mostly need practice and instruction with irregular verbs, which follow no rules, and the various individual quirks of their mother tongue. What kids have more trouble with is the shifting, or evolving, parts of language.

Although parents and teachers also struggle to teach "correct" grammar and pronunciation, they are fighting a natural tendency for language to change over time. Languages are born, evolve, and then die, and people are always adding or subtracting words or changing how they are used.[34] Kids do great with the basics of structure, but they need to be taught the more slippery edges of dialect, slang, and the current "correct" form.

Most parents in Western culture initiate talking to their kids in a language dubbed "Motherese" in which sentences are simplified and repetitive, and invariably mostly questions. What is this? What do you want? Are you tired? Baby hungry? And parents believe that the child will learn or improve his or her language by answering these questions or imitating the words. And because many kids practice their language by mimicking adults—Q. Do you want this toy? A. Ooy—parents presume practice makes perfect. But it is development, which cannot be hurried or slowed down with verbal gymnastics by parents, that commands when and how kids talk. And this has nothing to do with smartness. There is no correlation between early verbalization and IQ or later achievement in any realm. In other words, kids who talk relatively early end up no smarter than kids who talk relatively later.[35]

But lest parents think they have no role in language development, there are significant verbal arenas in which environment (that is, parents, community, peers, school, and culture) makes a major difference. Without interaction, there is no language. The basic importance of verbal exposure was dramatically confirmed in 1970 when a thirteen-year-old girl named Genie was brought to linguistic experts for evaluation.[36] Genie had been imprisoned in a room by her father since she was eighteen months old, and no one was allowed to speak to her. After escaping with her mother, Genie was suddenly exposed to language and she quickly learned how to talk—but only to a limited degree. She was supposedly of normal intelligence, and yet her talking went no further than that of a young child. She could make five-word sentences that made sense, but these sentences were simple and without any ambiguity. She also had trouble with verb tenses, although she understood their meaning. Linguist Derek Bickerson says that Genie acquired her language much like a chimpanzee, or a two-year-old child, and she just couldn't get past that.[37] The parts of her brain that would have been open to language had developed past the stage when acquisition is easy. She was like a person learning a new language, or someone making up a pidgin language, and she was arrested at that stage. And so exposure to language, by parents or others, is clearly critical for more advanced talking.

The influence of environment on language is multifaceted.

Obviously, kids need to grow appropriately and be well nourished, healthy, and attentive. And they need to be part of a social environment in which the context for speech and understanding language is provided. In that sense, language moves from mere words and syntax to communication among people, and this is where parents, schools, and communities play a part. Kids might know how to produce words in the right order and make sense of what others say, but obviously the context for those words and the richness in which they are communicated is just as important. Saying what you mean, using the right words and phrases for the right situation, being able to understand what others say, is a complex acquired *social* skill, not just a linguistic skill, and it must be learned.[38]

The verbal environment in which language is acquired can deeply affect how a child communicates relative to the societal norm. Children who read a lot have bigger vocabularies. Children who grow up in homes where conversation is always going on will reflect that environment and use language in complex and varied ways. The children of parents with a higher educational level achieve higher verbal scores on standardized tests. Kids who hear mostly imperative sentences—"Don't do that"—also end up lower on the verbal scale than those who hear more varied speech. More significant, these differences are already entrenched by age three.[39] When the context for communicating is rich, the child speaks and hears in rich ways; when that context is more sparse, the child hears and understands the basics but without elaboration. As a result, communication with those who might be more skilled is awkward.[40]

But the relationship between family environment and verbal

competence is more complex than tests might assume. For example, the educational and socioeconomic background of parents may be implicated in how well kids use words, but well-educated, high-status people are not necessarily masters of social language. White middle- and upper-class homes are typically nuclear family homes, and so household conversation is often limited to dyads. Such conversation is often less frequent than in extended family homes—there just aren't that many people around, compared with homes or cultures where there is extended family and privacy and time alone is less important. Children in middle-class or affluent households often spend a lot of time alone and may not get as much practice in the art of interpersonal conversation. Interestingly, academic studies on the relationship between parental education and social status and a child's verbal skills have, of course, focused on differences in overall vocabulary and effect on IQ (important factors to upper-class academics), but not on the interpersonal competence of these different groups.

What seems to count most is exposure to language, both verbal and written. In the West, we tend to sequester our kids into specific age groups. A richer verbal atmosphere, of course, would be multi-age groups where little children will pick up the vocabulary, and verbal skills, of older children. Also, spending time around a variety of adults is always a good learning experience. Instead of putting our children to bed early when friends come over, we might let them join in the party, conversing with adults as part of a normal evening. And, of course, reading to children on a regular basis also shows them the beauty of language and storytelling. Children's reading groups at the local library, where they might see other children quietly listening, is also good reinforcement.

But more than anything, just talking to kids, letting them hear you talk to others, is the traditional way in which children learn not just words but how to communicate.

It's also important to note that it's not just the parental atmosphere that has an effect on how kids talk. Cultural ideology, which directs what parents say to their kids from the moment of birth on, also has a dramatic influence on the development of speech. For example, we in the West love to chat with our babies. From the moment they are born, we hold them up to our faces and yak away. But this urge to talk with infants is not universal. In many cultures, the very idea that you chat with babies is silly. The Gusii in western Kenya, for example, don't talk to their babies like we do. In fact, the Gusii are convinced that if you spend all that time chatting up your kids, they will grow to be selfish and self-centered adults. The Gusii also recognize that children learn language perfectly fine without being "talked to" or "taught." And since Gusii toddlers are always carried and always engulfed in a social milieu, they hear plenty of talk.[41] It's just that mothers see no reason to talk to them as if they were conducting vocabulary and grammar drills.

No matter what culture kids grow up in, the range of how well and how early kids start to talk is magnificently varied, as varied as most developmental stages. Some children form words before they are a year old, while others speak not a word until they are two. My daughter and her little friend were born two days apart. At twenty-one months, they were almost exactly the same height, the same weight, and seemed to be at the same cognitive point—both understood verbal commands and comments and knew exactly what was being said to them. But they were very different when it came to verbalization. One had been mimicking adult words for months, while the other had a much smaller vocabulary and was just beginning to mimic. Interestingly, the one who was less verbal was the more physically able kid, the one running and jumping who never fell down, while the more verbal kid was less sure on her feet. But by the time they were three, there was no difference—both had a rich vocabulary and wanted to talk all the time. It's no surprise that these two good friends expressed a verbal difference. Experts claim that there is at least a year difference among kids in when they start to talk and that, even then, how they talk takes different paths.

More significant, children are born expecting a response to their early utterances. Communication is conducted among people, and kids instinctively know this; they respond to live human voices, but not to recorded ones or voices from the television.[42] At six months, babies can distinguish among phonemes, the smallest units of the sound palate that make up human speech. Babies can also discriminate among those sounds and focus on which ones are significant for their language.[43]

Between five and seven months, as all parents know, babies begin to play with sound—they coo and gurgle, babble and shout. By eight months, they usually make syllablelike sounds that are the same in all languages. A sort of gibberish appears at about one year of age. From there on out, experts say, language is acquired by experience and experimentation.[44] Around eighteen months, language acquisition speeds up, although this can be much later for many kids. This is also the developmental point where a second or even third language is easily incorporated, because the neural pathways are still being formed. As young children start to pick up words and articulate them, they seem to acquire a new one every few hours. Somewhere between the ages of two and three, kids go through a period of incremental language acceleration. By four years of age, they pretty much have it down and only need to figure out irregular verbs and tricks of their native tongue.[45] And by the age of five, they can read a few words and begin to comprehend the words on a page.[46]

Experimentation throughout language acquisition is, of course, flavored by culture. Kids in English-speaking countries realize that word order is important in English; in other languages, intonation or clicks or nasal sounds are key.[47] Chinese kids understand that raising or lowering the pitch of a word changes its meaning. !Kung San kids of Botswana become adept at clicking their tongues against various parts of the mouth to make a word. French-speaking children become masters of nasal sounds, and German kids can throw off sounds from deep in their throats. Cultural quirks of pronunciation are learned.

What is so remarkable about human forms of communication is that they are so complex and yet fundamentally innate. Learning to talk is one of the tasks of children, and kids must talk to become really human. But within that broad framework of language acquisition, there is great variation, especially during the early years. What all the research points to is individual variation in the first few years but a compelling drive to talk. And that overall language skills cannot be speeded up, although they can be enriched in later childhood. And so have no linguistic expectations of your child for the first three years because there is no way to tell if your particular child will begin to talk at age eighteen months or a year later. And there is nothing you can do to push them verbally. Being patient and allowing them to acquire language at their own pace makes for the best verbal atmosphere of all. And then you can expect a three-year-old to make sentences that you and others can understand.[48] Don't worry, that chatty child is just around the corner.

And as kids soon learn, how you talk and what you say is important. It determines your options in life, it forms your identity, it charts your path. Intersecting into the biology of language is the culture of language. Kids pick up on how to talk relatively easily. More difficult to comprehend is how a culture's language colors one's world.

The Anthropology of Language

Cows say *moo;* ducks say *quack;* pigs say *oink;* roosters say *cockadoo-dledoo.* At least in American English. In Germany, the cow might say *muh,* but roosters say *kikeriki* and chickens say *put put put.* In Puerto Rico, children learn that cows say *muh,* roosters say *qui-qui-ri-ki,* and pigs make a snorting sound that can't be written down. Children of the Kiapo Indians of the Amazon learn that chickens say *ak kren ayan* and ducks say *wayn wayn.*

Ask any adult in language different from your own what cows and pigs and ducks and chickens say, and you'll get a plethora of livestock noises and a lot of laughs. The answers are often onomatopoeic (that is, the words are fashioned after the noises animals make), but interestingly, each culture translates those sounds a bit differently. Language is, in fact, also an integral part of culture, and so it differs among cultures.

There are currently about sixty thousand languages in the world, and umpteen dialects within each of those languages. As humans have crossed the globe, as they formed exclusive cultural groups, they also fractured into all these languages. Anthropologists, of course, have been fascinated by language and how it colors our world. In fact, many cultural anthropologists think that talking is so much a part of who we are that language also *forms* who we are (that is, the words we use also construct our world).[49] This traditional view, often called linguistic relativism, comes from a time when scholars in the West believed that humans were born as blank slates and that everything we know has to be learned. A more recent version says that the ability to speak and listen is clearly driven by biology, but then culture, society, and individual behavior intersect with that ability, and thus we have a cultural Tower of Babel that filters everything we do and think.

Anthropologists Elinor Ochs and Bambi Schieffelin, who have studied speech acquisition in several cultures, point out that as caretakers talk to kids in certain ways, more than language is being molded.[50] They contend that *how* caregivers talk to kids varies across cultures, and that this verbal landscape makes a major difference in how people grow up and view the world. As such, language is a major aspect of socialization, one that is accomplished through words.

Anthropologists have used language to get at what people think, who they feel they are, and how they run their lives. For example, kinship terms are a staple of ethnographic work. Any anthropologist worth his or her salt knows that by interviewing people about the terms traditionally used for mother and child, and then branching out, you can learn a lot about culture. Very quickly, you understand which relationships have power, what the mating system might be, and who is connected to whom and why. You might even get a decent picture of how the entire social system works. Kinship is also safe territory—everyone likes to talk about their relatives. Anthropologists are also interested in how subjects, such as gender, social status, and economic activity, are described by language.[51] This is why ethnographic work relies not just on watching people but asking questions and listening to what people say as well.

And not surprising, language is important for those interested in children across cultures because it is through language that kids become socialized and become functioning members of a society. Words are used every minute to teach children who they are and how to behave, what is acceptable and what is not. Language and how kids acquire the social rules of conversation tell the story of a culture.

Most kids in Western culture learn to talk in a dyadic, one-on-one, sort of way. Studies of white middle-class toddlers show that the most frequent arena of chat is between mother and child, the primary linguistic dyad. Mothers typically spend a lot of time looking babies and young kids in the eyes and talking to these kids as if they were full-fledged conversational partners.[52] I do this myself. From the moment my daughter was born, I chatted with her all through her infancy. I had a running one-sided conversation with her and asked how she was, talked about my day, gave her a label for every object—car, book, cookie, Mommy. And when she began to babble back, I spent much of the day asking her what I thought were simple questions. We'd stand in the kitchen together with no one else around and chat, or at least I would chat.

Mostly, I'd ask over and over, "Cookie?" "What about a toy?" And when she didn't answer, I adjusted those questions to her level, guessing what she might say if she could. "Want cookie?" "Toy?" And when she began to mumble words back at me, I spent a lot of time listening hard and trying to interpret what she might be saying, as if she had just arrived from a foreign country and only had rudimentary knowledge of English.

What I didn't know at the time was that this style, which felt so natural and normal to me, is decidedly Western, white, and middle-class. Our verbal interaction was dyadic and kid-oriented. I felt compelled to label everything around her with words, as if this were the secret to speech. And I became her translator. As Ochs and Schieffelin point out, setting up the dialogue like this is how we Westerners parent in general. We accommodate to the child, rather than expecting the child to accommodate to the adult level. We have special clothes and food and books for kids, and generally separate them off from the adult social world. The medium may be language, but the cultural message is clear—being a kid in white middle-class America means being separate from adults in this society. We accommodate to their level, at least for a time, which confirms for them that they are the center of attention.

Other cultures talk and interact with their preverbal kids in very different ways. Bambi Schieffelin spent years in New Guinea living with the Kaluli people, a nonliterate society where people make a living in the tropical rain forest by fishing, hunting, and growing crops.[53] Villagers used to reside in one long house, but these days extended families live in a smaller house together. Kids, then, are part of a multi-age extended family group in which conversation is never private. And yet conversation is extremely important to Kaluli life. As Schieffelin says, "Everyday life is overtly focused around verbal interaction. Kaluli think of, and use, talk as a means of control, manipulation, expression, assertion, and appeal. Talk gets you what you want, need, or feel you are owed."[54] This philosophy comes out in how kids are taught to talk. Mothers don't stare at their infants and chat with them as I did because they (correctly) feel that babies don't understand. Instead, mothers turn babies toward others and then speak for the baby in what is really a three-way conversation. And they don't use baby talk but aim the verbalization at the level of the other speaker—if it's an older child, she becomes a ventriloquist for the baby in a high-pitched voice but verbalizes at the child's level. And so the conversation is really between mother and older child, and the baby is not really part of a dyad as they are in the West. While the baby is not a talking partner, it is engulfed in all this chat, even more so than a child growing up in a nuclear family household where talking is mostly dyadic.

Kaluli children become major players in the conversational milieu once they have uttered two significant words: "mother" and "breast." Mothers then begin directing their speech at kids, asking questions and presenting declarative sentences, demanding the child repeat what is said using the word *elema* after each phrase, which means, "Say like that." Schieffelin gives an example. MOTHER: "Whose is it? Say like that. Is it yours? Say like that." And these examples usually involve a third person as part of the interaction. More interesting, labels for objects, a verbal achievement which is so important in the West, is not an issue. Instead, mother tells the child what she wants to hear and the child is expected to accommodate to adult ways, not the other way around. They also correct the child's use of language, pushing them to talk like adults. At the same time, Kaluli adults avoid interpreting what the child might be saying because in this culture they believe that one can never know what another thinks. Kaluli never gossip and they make sure that when referring to what someone else said that the source of the information is revealed.

Kaluli society, Schieffelin explains, is egalitarian and everyone is of equal status. Language serves the purpose of reinforcing that everyone is equal. And so the cultural values of negotiating with direct adult speech, but not projecting into what others say, are passed along in the way language is taught to children. As Schieffelin puts it, children are "learning language and learning from language."[55] Through language, kids learn about the pace of conversation, about when to be autonomous and when to be connected, that relationships are built over time, and how to become an integrated member of a small social group that's tightly connected.

These two contrasting examples, the white middle-class Western model and the Kaluli, are but an illustration of how the acquisition of language is intimately entwined with the acquisition of culture.[56]

The Politics of Kidspeak

Language is power. As we speak, as we choose certain words, knowing that those words have meaning, and sometimes that meaning, depending on the speaker, the listeners, and the context, can alter everything. Kids also learn the power of language early; it is part of their socialization. Parents, peers, schools, community all have a role in shaping what kids say by judging what is acceptable and what is not. This process begins at home as parents correct grammar and word choice, and as they speak as role models. There are swearwords and dirty words and good words and happy words. There are words that are fine at home, but not fine in public. And kids learn that the rules of speaking and conversation are shifting rules and that the smart kid knows exactly when to change his or her pattern of speech.

Anthropologists are especially interested in how language interacts with a person's sense of identity—specifically, how language informs such issues as gender and status. Although some think such social issues come later in life, others believe that these issues are integrated into language aimed at kids from the moment they are born.[57] The way caretakers speak to babies, some suggest, models much of acceptable behavior. American mothers chat endlessly with babies, for example, unconsciously giving the message that the baby is an individual and worthy of such attention. Gusii mothers of western Kenya feel that such verbal attention produces an adult that will be self-centered and selfish and not fit into the family system, and so they do not chat with their babies.[58] Kaluli mothers engage their babies in three-way discussions, setting the example that life is a series of multifaceted, not individual or dyadic, interactions.[59] In each style, the societal goals as well as the path to individual identity is set.[60]

Gender and status, at least in Western society, are entwined, and kids not only learn this early, they echo what adults do. Mothers and fathers, research shows, talk differently to kids, which in turn models how they talk. In the West, fathers speak in imperative sentences twice as often as mothers. Thirty percent of the time that these dads talk to their little kids they give imperative directions, such as "Don't go there," and they talk that way more often to boys than girls. Western mothers typically speak in longer sentences, and ask more indirectly than directly, and they speak the same to boys and girls, at least in this dimension.[61] In one study of five-year-olds and language use, children used puppets to act out roles of family members. Father puppets, as directed by the kids, talked in commands. Mother puppets spoke in baby talk, talked sweetly, and asked rather than commanded. Mother puppets also gave reasons for their requests.[62] And kids mimic these roles; boys utter more imperatives themselves, while girls often respond to imperatives by ignoring them.[63] In one study concentrating on how a two-year-old used directives, researchers found that the child, who had just acquired language, was already savvy to status and gender issues. She used imperatives with fellow two-year-olds but was much more solicitous when speaking with four-year-olds. She also differentiated by speech when talking to her mother or father; she was repetitious with her father and more polite with him.[64] Such early awareness of status and role is found in other cultures as well.[65]

In cultures where children attend school, they further learn about status and their position in that hierarchy and how their gender influences that position. And they learn that what might be acceptable at home is not necessarily valued at school.[66] Most parents have faith that schools are teaching "correct" grammar and proper speaking and writing styles. But what the schools teach is only what a small body of individuals, the school board, have decided is acceptable. All other styles, vocabularies, and grammars are considered wrong and of less value. This produces a societal norm that is then imposed on everyone, regardless of their background. In one sense, such a collective approach is good because it provides a common form of communication. On the other hand, having one acceptable way to talk discounts significant changes in any language that are ongoing.

Children are, in fact, quite good at learning two distinct languages and all the appropriate usage that comes with two kinds of talking. For example, many children in the United States speak one language at home and another at school, and they are able to switch back and forth with abandon. They do this with such ease that parents should realize that it is possible for children to hold on to both these languages and their cultural context at the same time. Kids need not give up one tongue for another. They are also able to move among two or more forms of a language, different accents or colloquialisms; with time, experience, and a little cultural instruction, they learn what words are okay in which context. Children, in other words, are highly malleable when it comes to the use of language.

An imposed standard should be recognized as such, neither a right nor a wrong way to talk and write, but an agreed-upon standard that has no intrinsic value in and of itself. In fact, we might understand that when kids arrive at school with all sorts of languages and all sorts of language styles, that this plethora of words and styles is one of the amazing abilities of humans, rather than a deficit that needs to be corrected as soon as possible.

Humans see the world through a linguistic lens, as well as other lenses of the senses. We know who we are as we form the words to describe ourselves, and we know we belong most fundamentally when we speak the same language. Biology has given us the ear, mouth, throat, and brain capacity for speaking and hearing. Culture, community, family, and parents have then shaped that language to construct a meaningful world for each of us. Human language has been selected by evolution because for many reasons, being able to communicate in this way has helped our ancestors survive and reproduce. At this point in human evolution, we need language. For kids, learning to talk, being able to express their thoughts, is perhaps the most magical stage of development and the one that makes them human.

CHAPTER FIVE

What Kids Know

I recently visited our local toy store, a place called Creative Kids. It's billed not as a toy shop per se, but a store where parents can find the tools they need to make their kids learn, make their kids smart. I suspected it wasn't like the toy stores of my youth, where dolls and stuffed animals competed for space with building blocks, and I was right. There are some dolls, way in the back, but most of the floor space is taken up with more complicated items, more sophisticated and technical stuff. There's a wall of puzzles made out of wood, felt, or some sort of squishy stuff alongside a mountain of snap together figures, all with directions on how to put these things together correctly. And there's another wall overcome with sets of plastic figures that make up various tableau— boxes filled with scenes from the farm, the sea, a castle, or downtown—a whole civilization played out in colored figures. One side of the store is reserved for science projects and magic tricks, so ant farms live close to rabbits out of the hat. And there are train sets and car sets of every material and size and ways to set them up and take over a room. What I saw everywhere was busyness.

The anthropologist in me couldn't help but stand in awe at all these consumer goods, all targeted to make us parents feel inadequate—if we don't buy that puzzle, will our four-year-old be able to sort by size and color? If we don't get them hooked on science at five, is there no hope for their advancement? Should I buy that train set to make sure my daughter understands the intricacies of transportation? And will she have the mental capacity and manual dexterity to lay the track and put together the cars like the box says she should at her age?

Creative Kids, I must admit, gave me a headache because like all parents, I want my kid to learn how to read, write, and communicate. I want her to function in the world as a thinking being. And I wonder how in the world she will learn to do that. Actually, I wonder how *I* learned all that. How do any of us grow from spaced-out toddlers, children who can apparently only understand simple commands, to adults who know so much?

How Kids Think

Thinking is a complicated endeavor. And for humans, how we think is especially complex. Our kind of knowing includes a long list of mental abilities, such as perceiving what is around us and then processing that information, setting rules of behavior, classifying what we see and feel, remembering, thinking about ourselves, making decisions, and of course, dreaming. We also not only perceive the world around us, but we have this thing called consciousness, although no one has been able to really describe what consciousness is—we all just know that we are conscious beings.

Scientists call this whole mental conglomeration "cognition."[1] And what an amorphous concept this is. Although there have been endless volumes written to describe each of these abilities, and any number of demonstrations detailing the process of thought, no one is really sure how the mind really works. No one yet really knows what consciousness is, how memory is encoded and retrieved, or how thoughts pass through the brain and translate into action. In fact, the brain is surely one of the big mysteries of science. And so researchers have also had a field day trying to chart how mentality develops, how kids start out thinking like kids but grow to think like adults. The idea is that if researchers could document the process over time as a human grows, they might better understand how it works in the first place. For parents, knowing how kids think at various stages is also important. Everyone, especially parents, is interested in figuring out how outside influences can alter, for better or worse, how that process unfolds. Can we make a better, smarter, more thoughtful child?

Studying, or even tracking, mental development is complicated. It's impossible to really know exactly when the baby or child begins to "understand" something. We know that infants feel and react, and they seem to "know" the important people in their lives. But at some point, parents begin to notice that the baby is paying attention in a different sort of way, watching with big eyes and apparently absorbing, as if they were taking everything in and trying to make sense of it. And they are, but scientists have no idea how this really works. We only know, as parents and as researchers, that eventually the baby responds in ways that suggest some sort of thought was involved, as if a light turned on. I vividly remember when my daughter, at twenty months old, grabbed a wooden spoon and used it to fish out a magnet that had slipped under the refrigerator. No one had taught her to do that and she had never observed Mommy using a spoon that way—she simply put two and two together. But I recognized that puzzle solving skill for what it was—a leap in mentality. These leaps are constrained, that is helped and hindered, by physical growth and physical coordination. My daughter could do the spoon trick because at twenty months she could easily squat down, focus on the magnet, reach for a wooden spoon, and sweep the spoon under the fridge. And then she could stand and play with the fridge magnet, something she was unable to do a year before. And so one of the complications of understanding mental ability is recognizing that physical ability is implicated—both are entwined in the developmental process.

Another complication of learning to think like a human, or to think about thinking like a human, is language. How we conceive of the development of mentality is also often connected with the development of language. Clearly, before they can talk, kids know things and are mentally processing, but through language we figure out what they truly understand (see Chapter Four). And by putting names to things, by communicating their thoughts, kids also exercise their thinking. And so language (that is, expressing oneself in words) becomes integral to consciousness, knowing, thinking, memory, and learning—every mental process, except perhaps unconscious thought, is somehow colored by words.

At the very soul of human thought is symbolism, and kids attain symbolic meaning very early.[2] By two years of age, children know and act out that various objects are not just what they are but also representations of other things—a bowl is not just a bowl but also can be a hat. They can, in other words, invent as well as understand that there might be a relationship between an object and an idea that has nothing to do with the actual function of the object. As adults, we do this every minute of every day; to be symbolic is to think. But pause and consider what it really means to be able to do this kind of mental manipulation. I thought about this transition to real thought every time I read my infant daughter a book. I would say, "Here is a duck. Well, it's not really a duck but a picture of a duck. And this word for duck is not really a duck or a picture of a duck but some letters that mean duck. You know, that quacking thing at the park." I didn't want to lie or misrepresent what I was showing her, and so I found myself wading, like an existential duck, into deep waters. But by the time she was two, I found there was no real need to get so twisted up about all this— she "knew" that the drawing of the fuzzy yellow thing on the page was just like the thing at the park because she called both of them ducks.

Kids take this symbolic ability and use it for play. They use rocks for dolls, which in turn represent living people. They begin to draw circles that approximate heads and add eyes to them. By the time they are two, kids are masters at manipulating symbols in their play. At first, parents find such behavior amazing—to watch a child for the first time put a doll to bed, smoothing the cover and kissing it good night, is one of the sweetest things on Earth. But soon, this kind of symbolic play becomes routine. We often call it "imagination" and encourage our kids to take that symbolic play as far as it can go—play house, play doctor, play camping.

Children also exercise their mentality when they imitate others. Kids begin to imitate as babies, although it is hard to determine that such imitation is purposeful. But even before one year of age, kids pick out specific acts to imitate. They might repeat similar verbal expressions or repeat a pattern of behavior that Mommy does. The miracle is that none of this imitation is purposefully taught or learned, it just happens. Two-year-olds can push the TV remote or talk on the phone. They empty the dishwasher or act like they are driving. We are both charmed by these behaviors, because it is unpredictable which ones the kids will pick up on, and amused because they usually do them so badly. And it is simply amazing when little kids imitate some behavior they have seen weeks ago. Research on two-year-olds in Western culture, where Mother is the primary caretaker, shows that imitation is most often of Mother.[3] Presumably, imitation in other cultures where there are other primary caretakers would follow who the child sees most often.

The ability to imitate has been considered one of the markers of human intelligence. But other animals imitate. Some birds, for example, are expert imitators. Myna birds can imitate the human voice using a very different vocal apparatus and other species mock each other.[4] But this kind of copying, researchers believe, has nothing to do with intelligence per se. Such a skill is aimed at survival, or a trick to gain food or space or mates. Imitation at this level is singular, focusing on one act or task, one bit of information. Psychologist Richard Byrne of St. Andrews University in Scotland says that there are levels of imitation that do indicate higher levels of intelligence and that only dolphins, great apes, and humans seem to imitate at what he calls the "program level." He means that the imitator not only "gets" the bits and pieces that make up the whole task, they also "get" that there is a cohesive plan, a goal, and they imitate all the steps to complete the action. Great apes (that is, chimpanzees, gorillas, and orangutans, as well as humans) are the only ones who imitate at this program level. And at least for humans, we know how mentally complex this kind of imitation can be. It means you have to place yourself in the mind of another, to understand both the cause and effect of each small action, and follow in sequence a coherent plan to reach a goal. Think of tying shoes, or putting on clothes, or making juice—all things that kids "learn" to do by imitating others. Without instruction, without a word, they often just start doing things that others do. And this seemingly simple behavior is a sign of how smart they are, how finely evolution has preprogrammed the human brain to imitate and learn.

Kids are also intelligent because early on they can solve problems (that is, they see a problem and think through a solution, and they often do this without trial and error). Scientists call this ability "insight." Sometimes what seems like insight, a sudden answer floating to the surface to solve a problem, is really the result of the mind muddling the matter over. We could, as Byrne did when he asked subjects to think out loud when presented with a problem, actually demonstrate that what seems to be a sudden insight is really a long mental dance. Our minds usually operate all the time, experimenting with a long string of mental trial and error that ends in the right answer. But most often, the mind quietly goes about this kind of "thinking" about a problem, shooting off in tangents and back again, until the "Eureka!" answer becomes a conscious thought.

To do this, the brain must have memory, experience to draw on, and good observational powers. And humans, even little humans, are good at this. More important, the mind expands on this experience. Once we solve one problem, that experience is retained and used in some way in the future.[5] And this is why play is so important to kids. Play combines everything the mind needs to exercise—manual manipulation, props for imitation, the occasional "problem" to be solved, and varied experience.

Human intelligence has another property that develops as kids grow—the ability to know another's mind, the very essential idea that other people have thought and knowledge. Psychologists call this "theory of mind." We understand that others are also thinking beings and we "know" that those others might be thinking something different from our own thoughts. This knowledge is invaluable. To "know" that others "know" allows for all sorts of social interaction, everything from simple conversation to empathy.

Much of the work on theory of mind has been confirmed with work on autistic children, kids who apparently do not have a theory of mind. Autistic children think how they think and have no idea that others might think differently. They can't keep in their minds the fact that what they believe might not be what others believe, they cannot reconcile fact and belief. And little kids behave this way as well until they are about three and a half years old.

The classic experiment goes like this: Two adults are in a room with a small child. One adult puts a coin in a red box and leaves the room. While she is gone, the other adult takes the coin out and puts it in the green box and asks the child, "Where will the absent adult look for the coin?" A kid under four says, "In the green box," not realizing that since the first adult was not there to see the switch, her mind didn't register the change. The kid thinks all minds must think the same as hers does at all times. But over four years of age, the child knows that minds differ, and she recognizes that different information results in different knowledge and she says, "In the red box."[6]

There is some evidence that monkeys and apes might have some theory of mind. In lab experiments, they act like they have some idea that others think. And in the wild, they often act as if they are mind reading others. For example, low-status male baboons will sneak away from dominant males and lure females in their direction and mate. Clearly, those males "know" they are doing something that the dominant male would not allow. There are other cases of deception among nonhuman primates and other mammals, but humans are especially adept at this kind of mind reading—we do it every minute of every day.[7] In fact, knowing that others know is part and parcel of human interaction. But it is something that develops over time—babies are not born with this ability, they develop it. At first, babies rely on their own minds, but with time, they realize that what they think is not necessarily what Mommy thinks (see below).

And soon, this theory of mind bolsters the very concept of "self." Humans are not only conscious, they are self-conscious. We know that we exist, that each of us is an individual, that we are what we are. Studies of monkeys and apes show that they have the rudiments of this ability. In a series of experiments, chimpanzees, gorillas, and monkeys were set up to see if they had a concept of self. A mirror was placed in their cages and they were allowed to get used to the figure in the mirror. Then while asleep, researchers painted a bright red spot on the forehead of each animal. Upon waking, the chimp and gorilla looked in the mirror and reached up to wipe off the spot—suggesting they "knew" that the face in the mirror was their own. Only the monkey ignored the mark, as if the face in the mirror was another monkey, not them. Great apes, then, must have some sort of concept of "self," and so self-consciousness as a mental ability has roots as deep as our shared ancestry with apes.[8]

Using the same experimental protocol on human children, researchers have shown that kids under twenty-one months of age ignore the red spot on their noses. But around two years of age, they clearly show the concept of self-awareness by trying to rub the red spot off.[9] And simply by using the pronouns "I" and "mine," which they start to do about two years of age, we know that they have singled themselves out. Two-year-olds also express their sense of self when they give their opinions—and they seem to have an opinion about everything, as every parent of a toddler knows only too well. "I like it." "I don't like it." "I only want a blue one." They like certain things and don't others, are emphatic about it, and are happy to tell you so.

Knowing something about self is so integrated to being human that we are not particularly surprised when self is expressed verbally or in other ways—in fact, we expect it. But expressing self is actually a great mental leap and something that speaks to the fundamental intelligence of the human species.

As part of the theory of mind comes the ability to feel what others may feel (that is, empathy). Around two years of age, children begin to act as if they "know" what others feel. They look at and talk about babies who are crying, saying things like "Baby is sad." They comment when Mom or Dad looks unhappy. They frown when others frown. Such behavior suggests they not only feel things themselves, but they feel for others. Some have considered empathy a mark of the human species, but there is also indication that other primates have the roots of such empathy.

There are really two levels of recognizing the feelings of others. First is sympathy, the capacity of knowing that others have feelings. Little kids do this well. They recognize a happy face and a sad face; it is part of their social nature to be attuned to others and this ability develops early within the first two years. But empathy is something different. Empathy involves concern for the feelings of others, the ability to put oneself inside the mind of another and attempt to feel what they feel, sometimes actually doing something to alleviate the pain of others. This is a mental feat that serves social creatures, and humans are especially good at it. In fact, people who lack empathy for others are considered odd, antisocial, even pathological.

Primatologist Frans de Waal writes about various examples of sympathy and empathy in the animal kingdom in his book *Good-Natured*.[10] Sympathy is reasonably widespread. Animals, from dolphins to monkeys, show some sort of sympathy toward group mates who are sick and injured, and de Waal feels such feelings are expected in species in which relationships are based on long-term attachment; with attachment comes sympathy. Examples of empathy are more unusual. Elephants respond with despair to the death of one of their members; chimpanzees can die of grief. Watching a captive colony of chimpanzees and recording behaviors during and after a fight, animal behaviorist Michael Seres has shown that those not involved in the fight will comfort combatants after the fight is over.[11] They will touch and groom them, directing the most caring behaviors at those who are most upset. De Waal makes the case that chimpanzees, like no other animal except humans, go to a lot of trouble to seek out such comfort. "When upset," de Waal writes, "chimpanzees pout, whimper, yelp, beg with outstretched hand, or impatiently shake both hands so that the other will hurry and provide the calming contact so urgently needed."[12] Young chimps also throw temper tantrums to get attention and reassurance from others. And so the roots of empathy, and the urgent need for empathy from others, are part of our shared nature with at least chimpanzees.

We also know that empathy has relatively deep roots because the capacity for empathy develops early in humans—and on cue with other mental developments of children. Around two years of age, as they are developing all the other mental capacities, such as consciousness and self-awareness, kids become empathetic. And this makes evolutionary sense. We primates are designed to be highly social, even dependent on each other for survival. And you cannot depend on others unless you have an idea of what they are thinking and feeling (that is, theory of mind and empathy).

And so it is no surprise that these abilities develop early, that they are hard-wired, and that kids are quite good at both. But it is important to understand that all mental capacities are a product of both genes and experience. Most parents know that, and this is the arena in which we all wonder if we are doing what is best for the mental development of our children. Can we influence the development of particular mental capacities that we, as parents or as a society, deem "good"? Should our kids receive more mental stimulation, or stimulation of a particular kind? Should they be in social environments that foster sympathy and empathy? Or should we leave them alone to experience life as it unfolds?

Theories of Cognition

The "experts" certainly have a lot to say to parents about how to bring up a well-adjusted, smart child. Such theories begin with Jean Piaget, a Swiss psychologist who worked during the 1920s and was interested in how children think. In a sense, developmental psychology, the science of studying how kids reason, is based on Piaget's work. He believed that the process of cognition (that is, thinking and reasoning) was intimately tied to maturation. He began by watching his own children, and from there he tested various hypotheses about cognitive development with other children in the laboratory.

Piaget surmised that children don't think exactly like adults but that they develop through stages of mentality that could be charted. He believed that this developmental path was biological (that is, part of human nature). Piaget's ideas were echoed by a Russian scientist named Lev Vygotsky, who worked about the same time and also observed children and the parent-child relationship. Vygotsky emphasized even more than Piaget the idea that biology was instrumental in determining how children think and that human culture was part of human biology. He felt that anything cultural, including what parents do to teach their children by accident or design, is also, in a sense, biological, because absorbing that "environmental" layer is part of being human.[13]

The idea that both nature and nurture shape the way children think seems obvious to us these days, but it took more than thirty years for Piaget and Vygotsky's work to be appreciated. Instead, psychology, the science that studies how the mind works, was more influenced by Sigmund Freud, who saw children as small beings who only wanted their needs met, and B. F. Skinner, who thought kids were blank slates waiting to be taught.[14] But in the 1960s, the discipline of child development became a hot subject, and since then the theories of Piaget, Vygotsky, followed by a raft of other academics, have held forth about how children learn.

Step into any academic library and go to the section on children. Every university and college in the nation have courses in child development and there are as many good textbooks to match. Choose any one and thumb the pages of theory, developmental physiology, laboratory testing of kids' skills and abilities, and studies of children at home. What you discover in those pages are decades of academic work that will make your head spin. The children have been temporarily taken from their parents to test their anxiety level, set on ramps to check their coordination, faced with strangers to record their reaction, asked to name this or that object to figure out how they order the world, prompted to draw in order to allow researchers a window into their minds, and asked what they think. They have been measured, questioned, videotaped, recorded, and observed like, well, laboratory rats. And what have we learned? That infants and small children know more than some people thought; that there is a general pattern of development that takes young toddlers from not knowing much to being able to order their world with symbols and self; that kids don't reach the same mental or physical stage at exactly the same time; and that they are highly socially adept. There are lots more details in these works, but basically that's what we have learned.

Interestingly, any parent or parents who have had one child and have paid attention to their growth and development already know all this to be true. And those who have had more than one child have, in essence, been unintentionally running the same scientific protocols in their homes and coming up with the same results. Kids develop, grow, and learn along a similar but not singular path, and everything about them—their genes, their biology, their everyday and also unusual experiences, and who they interact with—makes a difference. And as parents, or citizens interested in children, we can exercise some control over this path by providing a healthy, safe, happy, and rich social environment. Child development research has been good because it focuses on children, shining the spotlight on the most vulnerable stage of the human life cycle and giving it some respect. But I also maintain that researchers have told us a lot of things we already knew and have sometimes let the theory overwhelm what kids really do. And they have focused way too much on white middle-class Western children—mostly in laboratory conditions—as if how those particular kids act in these artificial situations is the standard for human behavior.

From the more anthropological point of view, all of what these scientists have theorized about and tested makes evolutionary sense; some child development researchers, in fact, have recently incorporated the evolutionary view into their theories. Alison

Gopnik, Andrew Meltzoff, and Patricia Kuhl, in their book *The Scientist in the Crib,* in which they propose that young kids are like scientists in how they perceive and test what they see, write, "Evolution seems automatically to grant most children a fundamental capacity for intimacy, a profound psychological curiosity, and plenty of kinfolk to be intimate and curious about."[15] Their words echo a very new approach to childhood that asks how the path of development was molded by natural selection. Social abilities in children are part of our primate nature; learning right from wrong is necessary for long-term group living; self-consciousness may have been selected to keep our ancestors alive. And so the next step in child development research should move toward asking not *how* do kids think, but *why* do they and their adult counterparts think in certain ways?

How Do Kids Learn in Other Cultures?

A major assumption in child development is that kids all over the world are essentially the same. Are they?

In one classic work on West African children, older children were given a piece of paper and asked to draw a road. The kids drew two parallel lines, suggesting that they had no concept of perspective, that in the real world they had no idea of how things looked; if they had perspective, as any young artist knows, the lines would be wide at the bottom of the paper and narrow together toward the top of the paper. The researchers were surprised and decided to look at the way they had conducted the test. They soon found out that these kids, living in rural conditions without much of anything, had had no experience setting pencil to paper. And when the researchers explained how to use a pencil and how to translate things in a two-dimensional space, the kids caught on quickly—they immediately drew the road on paper as two open lines merging at the top of the paper. Testing method, not mental ability, was the problem.

When researchers move away from the lab, away from Western culture, which is clearly a culture of testing, they encounter all sorts of problems. Sara Harkness and Charles Super write of their experience working with Kipsigis children in western Kenya. Most of the non-Western research on child psychology has been conducted on African children, they point out, and yet African children are almost impossible to "test." In their work, they made sure the testing happened in a familiar atmosphere, where kids would be among friends and relatives, not restricted in any way. But it was impossible to get them to even repeat a simple story— which in the West would indicate a lack of attention, even low intelligence. "These kids are generally healthy and well nourished," Harkness and Super protest. "In everyday circumstances they can be as active and vocal as children anywhere, swinging from the rafters of a maize storehouse, boisterously roughhousing, or gleefully teasing a goat. . . . Why does the testing situation, even the most friendly and familiarized version of it, produce such inhibition of thoughtful response?"[16] The answer, the researchers believe, lies at the very heart of how Kipsigis kids are raised and how they learn.

Kipsigis do not ascribe to the parental ideology of independence and self-reliance that American parents hold so dear. Instead, children are expected and trained to be obedient, responsible

members of an entwined household. In that capacity, they are expected to soon take on child-care tasks and domestic chores. And
unlike the nuclear family system in which both parents tend to be
emotionally close to the children, Kipsigis fathers are quite distant,
and after infancy, Kipsigis mothers are also relatively distant. That
distance is required in a system in which the hierarchy is clear—
adults are in charge and children must obey and fit into the overall
family arrangement.

This push for obedience, respect, and responsibility among
the Kipsigis coincides with the process of language acquisition
and can be seen in how mothers talk to their little kids. They
rarely talk to them and take no active role in teaching them how to
talk as Western parents do; they talk primarily by command. "Get
water." "Pick up the baby." As Harkness and Super point out, the
main response to an imperative is action, not a verbal response,
and so kids learn very early how *not* to talk; kids learn that appropriate behavior in front of an adult is silence, not chat. In other
words, understanding their mothers, not talking back to them, is
what is important for the Kipsigis child. And this works into a
Western way of testing these kids. No matter how friendly the atmosphere, children will not speak to adults because that is unacceptable behavior. In fact, the researchers suggest that the best
testers for African children would be other children. Maybe then
they could get some idea about mental abilities of these children.

The point is, the tests we are most familiar with—IQ, various
personality and temperament tests, which we assume are acceptable ways to figure out how all kids think and act—are too culturally laden to be models for children everywhere. This study also
underscores the power of culture in promoting, featuring, and pro-

ducing those aspects of "intelligence" which are favored in each culture. Western culture favors self-expression and highly verbal children and adults, other cultures favor other human characteristics. And so when we think about what our kids learn, and the path and speed at which they learn it, we have to be careful to realize that we are only focusing on a small subset of knowledge and expression. They might learn to repeat numbers, identify colors, name objects, and we might think they are so smart for being able to do this. But this kind of "intelligence" is but a small fraction of what kids learn and know.

The way we view the process of learning also has an effect on our value judgments about intelligence. In the West, we believe that children must be taught and that the best way to teach them is a school where a trained teacher works with a collective of same-age children. This idea of school is so ingrained that no parent would question that children go to school—how else could they learn? But the concept of a formal "school" is historically rather recent, linked to the industrial revolution when children were sent to official schools to learn how to work in factories—or as a place to put them when their mothers went to work.[17] Interestingly, the new movement for home schooling, with parents as the teachers, is often considered "odd" or "scandalous" because these kids are not learning in what is now considered "normal" conditions, as if kids only learn when they are sitting in a classroom, faced by a teacher who imparts knowledge. Clearly, there are other ways to learn, and different philosophies about learning.

Among the Piri, a Polynesian village community that lives by fishing and small plot farming, adults believe that children learn by themselves.[18] The path of learning, they believe, follows maturation, and when there are differences among children in their abilities, they must be innate. As anthropologist Robert Levy says of the Piri belief system about children and learning, "No one teaches them very much."[19] Parents tolerate a lot of trial and error and only correct children when they are in danger. But it's not as if the children are left to themselves. Parents still give guidance. But their essential belief is that kids do it on their own and in their own time. Children are expected to watch closely, and to mimic adults, and they are expected to achieve various things by certain ages—those who do not are shamed. But over all, we would see this kind of approach as negligent, because we don't share this belief system. Instead, Westerners believe solely in active teaching, and could not tolerate allowing a child to learn simply by watching or mimicking.

Robert LeVine, who has studied the Gusii, a population of small plot horticulturists in western Kenya, for forty years, makes the point that how a people make a living constructs the traditional, accepted, learning environment. For Gusii children, until very recently when schools became popular, the home was the place of learning.[20] Since the Gusii marry polygynously (that is, each man will have several wives), home means several women and their children living in a compound. Within that compound are children of several ages, all of whom have domestic chores. Each stage of development, according to the Gusii, is linked to certain tasks, and when a child does that task well, it means he or she is of high moral character. Kids are expected to be obedient, listen to commands, do what they are told, and be a good child. Young children run errands, older children work in the fields. They all do domestic chores that would amaze Western parents.

Gusii kids learn how to do these tasks by being part of the work. At first they watch and do small parts and as their skills and abilities grow, their responsibility for the task grows. LeVine calls this "participatory learning." For example, boys tag along while their older brothers herd the family cattle and soon they are in charge. The parental role in all this is to observe their progress and give corrective feedback, and sometimes that feedback is harsh, according to LeVine. "Neither parents nor older siblings provide praise, approval, or other rewards for correct performance of desired tasks," he writes.[21] To the Gusii, such praise would undermine the household hierarchy; they believe such praise would make a child conceited and unmanageable. And they feel any child will be motivated by the desire to be like the older children and that mothers need not provide any other motivation to get the children to behave.

Learning at School

Learning in most industrialized nations is thought to happen by instruction from adult to child, and mostly at school. But not all Western cultures implement this kind of learning in the same way. Each country, in fact, thinks that learning must occur in a particular way.

In Israel, for example, citizens believe that child care and education are the responsibility of the collective. Israeli families are provided free child care, health benefits, and leave. Parents believe that kids as young as two years old should spend some time in a group situation. They feel that to be home alone with Mother all the time is neither normal nor natural and that child development requires a group setting.[22] By 1982, 67 percent of two-year-old and 92 percent of three-year-old Jewish Israelis were in either day care or nursery school. Arab children, in contrast, are still raised primarily in the home in a family setting. The difference is based on a Jewish tradition that the community must care for individuals and that the collective is primarily responsible for the education of the young. As a result, institutionalized child care in Israel has become a vehicle for enculturation in a society that is made up of immigrants from many different cultures. As such, day care and preschool have become part of Israel's implementation of social identity.

Preschool in Japan, an industrialized nation with an ideology also geared toward the collective rather than the individual, takes on another form. Day care in Japan is primarily intended for working mothers and the poor; kindergarten is considered preparation for primary school. There are all sorts of nonparental care choices in Japan, from short-term "baby hotels" to day nurseries, which function like day care facilities, as well as preschools and kindergarten. Most are state-regulated and provide a uniformity of facilities. Like other cultures, the early years are more custodial, and the later years focused more on learning.[23] The real shift comes at kindergarten; in contrast with other industrialized nations, the primary function of kindergarten in Japan is social rather than cognitive.

Contrary to what someone in America might expect, Japanese kids in preschool spend the majority of their time in play, and this play is totally free-form and unsupervised. They sing, dance, exercise, or listen to a story as a collective only 15 percent of the day.

But they are encouraged to share, to play with others or build projects with others, and asked to share their experience during a class meeting. Various collective rituals throughout the day make the classroom a unit. Teachers use language that emphasizes the community of the class and make sure all the children are conscious of the effect of an individual's behavior on others. Teachers go to great pains to bring the individual into the collective, even during free play. In fact, the national guidelines for preschool include both autonomy and cooperation as moral goals, and downplay individual achievements.[24]

There is also a strong sense of order in Japanese preschools. Even in preschool, time tables are kept and the part of the day that is scheduled is divided in an orderly manner.[25] As anthropologist Eyal Ben-Ari noted, five-year-olds will be doing the same project at the same time all over the country. Moreover, it is a routine that doesn't vary over the years. Each Japanese child has the same experience, an experience that is mostly fun, rather than directed academic learning. The idea is to have fun together, but to also share, understand each other's emotions, and thus develop what child development researcher Catherine Lewis calls a "sense of purpose." Pressure to be good often comes from peers. In addition, teachers emphasize qualities such as empathy and pride in the group; they believe that intelligence can only be associated with self-control and good social behavior.[26] There are no isolated timeouts, nor are there any kids who do not want to participate in group activities.[27] Children who act up are not labeled as bad or noncooperative, but are encouraged by teachers and peers to join the group, thus reducing potential confrontations and encouraging kids to get along.

Learning in the school setting is thus run under different kinds of ideologies in different industrialized cultures. For example, in the United States, we think of preschool as a place to learn and that education should make up a big component. We assume this early education will help our youngsters as they enter grammar school, to become smart, educated, and successful individuals. For Israelis, preschool is a way to bring diverse backgrounds together. For the Japanese, early school is a moral lesson in getting along.

But we take this all on faith. School, or institutional learning, is one type of learning experience, one in which children sit quietly while an adult imparts knowledge in some way. In other cultures, without preschool, kids learn primarily as they play, work, or they follow adults around.

Examples across cultures highlight the fact that there are very different learning environments for children around the world. No one can say that one particular environment is "better" than another; each culture simply believes that "this is how it is done." But what would it be like if we in the West took our children out of school and expected them to imitate household chores and learn primarily by imitation? And what if cultures more attuned to learning by example rather than teaching sent their kids to school? Around the world, of course, the second experiment is taking place. Children who normally would be working for the family are now placed in rural schools, and as LeVine found out for the Gusii children, they do just fine in a more Western system of instruction. As the Gusii become more "Westernized," their children more often attend school and are faced with learning from one teacher, and they are acquiring skills that have nothing to do with what goes on at home. Although these kids were brought up to be obedient, silent, and are in no way used to the sort of teaching-learning chatty atmosphere of school, they do quite well. LeVine comments on the incredible resilience of kids and their ability to adapt to something that is so different from what they experience at home. Given a new learning environment, they adapt. And on the surface, anyone would consider education of this sort as "good," an opportunity to better one's self in the wider world. But there is a trade-off. As kids take on new belief systems, they are less able to fit into their family style. As such, this transition is indicative of the overall changes happening to lifestyles of rural people everywhere—the breakdown of family systems that functioned quite well, and the initiation of Western systems that don't yet make up for what has been lost. Mothers and children who used to spend much of the day together are now separated. Children are not there to do the chores that are so helpful to mothers. Most significant, small children don't have their elder siblings as babysitters and so mothers must find other caretakers or not finish much of their work at home and in the fields. These little kids, in turn, miss the interacting and learning from their older sibs. Also, much of what is now "learned" is delivered by teachers, who are not relatives, but authority figures backed by the government. By seeking education, which of course is a good thing, there have been major changes in how family systems run day to day and in the environment in which children develop. Families have had to adapt to these changes and accept the trade-offs and their consequences.

Lifelong Learning

School, teaching, reading, writing, computers, the Internet. All of this information seems important and all of us want our children to have the best possible atmosphere for learning. We assume that exposure to new and exciting ideas will do the trick, or that expensive schools and fancy toys will encourage kids to learn. If we were Gusii or Piri, we wouldn't think that way at all—we would simply go about our lives and figure the kids will catch on. But Westerners think differently. We believe that bringing up successful kids means they have to be smart in academic ways, and that means we have to buy them an education and make sure it sticks. Who is right? To my mind, there is tremendous sense to the Piri way. Most of the things my daughter does she learned herself, imitating her parents. She can wash dishes and fold laundry and she plays at her desk as if she were "working." She loves doing these things. Of course, we also teach her as well, correcting the way she holds scissors, asking her questions and seeking answers.

By looking at the way children in other cultures learn, I find myself questioning the accepted Western way. There is certainly a push these days to put our three-year-olds in preschool, make them ready for kindergarten and then grammar school. But this push for preschool, or for day care with "education" as a foundation, is quite new. When I was a kid just a generation ago, for example, there was no such thing as preschool. And I wonder what exactly we gain by institutionalizing our children so early. They learn all about what a classroom is, and what teachers do, but who exactly will they imitate and how will their social values form?

But in taking this view, I also am required to reject the way my culture views the learning process. I have to reject the idea that a high-powered school will make a child smart. I have to walk away from conversations in which parents discuss their kids' grades and test scores and not care if my child is not at the top of the class. I have to step back from the American sense of competition that is so familiar and become more relaxed about school and education and learning. I even have to have different standards of what is considered "success" in this culture. Then again, maybe a few years from now I won't have the conviction to bypass all that.

But I hope I retain the idea that learning is not something that just happens during the first three years, or only during childhood. Every day, for example, I learn something new, often things that change the way I think or feel or view life. I am sure this is true for you, too. Learning goes on constantly in all of us, sometimes gradually, sometimes constantly. And so maybe that is the most reasonable approach. Teach your children well, but also allow them to teach themselves and each other. Recognize that learning is not a limited quantity, or limited to a specific time in life. And that what our children don't learn today, they might just be able—and interested—in picking up in later years. Most of all, we need to enjoy the process of watching our children learn. This really isn't a competition, a race of who is smartest, or best, or most able. As parents, our job is to encourage the joy of learning something new, in our children and in ourselves.

CHAPTER SIX

Little Citizens

On Tuesdays and Thursdays, I take my daughter to The Tot Spot, a padded room filled with plastic cars and plastic slides where little kids can run around when there's a foot of snow on the ground. It's a wild place, but also lots of fun. Here she can interact with children of various ages—pet the babies, push the big boys, toss a ball to her best friend—or hang out and beg snacks from the other moms and dads. The Tot Spot is also a hotbed of socialization and morality.

A three-year-old boy pushes another kid. His mother runs over and grabs the little boy by the shoulders, turns him around, and explains, "This is not right, not good. Don't push your friend." She has clearly gone through this litany a zillion times, but she does it once more, clearly, patiently, trying to make a lasting impression but knowing that her son is barely paying attention. A two-year-old girl crowds the line for the slide; she hits the kid in front of her. The father of another kid tells her hitting is bad. And my daughter tries to supplant a smaller child from the plastic motorcycle. How pushy, I think, but wait to see what happens. The other kid moves off to another toy, but I worry that I should have intervened. And then my daughter trots up to other parents and begs food. I have pretzels and animal crackers with me, but no, she wants snacks from strangers. If she says "please" and "thank you" while scarfing up these treats, I feel somewhat vindicated, that at least she's a polite beggar.

All around The Tot Spot, lessons in what is right and wrong, the rules of polite society, are being imparted to these small citizens. The children are told hitting and pushing is bad, sharing is good, grabbing is bad, helping is good, biting is bad, hugging is good. And all the parents seem exhausted with stating what is obvious to adults—be nice, play nice.

The reason for lengthy human childhood, some say, is so that children can learn how to become adults. Implicit in this statement is that children must somehow "learn" adult behavior, that being a polite, caring adult is not innate. And just as implicit is the idea that someone has to teach them how to become adults— parents, other kids, community members, schools—that all of us have some input into how a child develops into a moral citizen who knows the rules and regulations of society. This kind of learning has nothing to do with the ordinary subjects taught at school, such as math and science, and more to do with becoming a citizen of a particular group.

It is a behavioral education.

Little Savages

Child psychologists give the name "socialization" to the process by which children acquire the rules of society.[1] And there is such a lot to learn. What to wear, what to say, how to talk, how to interact with different people—just about every minute of every day as an adult is framed by this or that social rule. More confusing, the rules can be different, depending on which part of society one is interacting with at the moment; kids learn early that what might be acceptable at home is not acceptable in school, for example. And how do they learn all this? By immersion and repetition.

The immersion part is easy to track. From the moment a baby is born, parental scripts outline a particular cultural and social world. These scripts, of course, don't appear from nowhere—each parent has expectations for their child, expectations that have been molded by tradition, experience, and of course, culture.[2] And then children are exposed to various groups that are part of that script. They may be part of an extended family that operates a certain way, or part of a nuclear family in which there are fewer members to interact with. They may attend day care with its charted rules or be with a nanny from another country who has a script that is very different from the parents.

Kids, of course, can accommodate all these confusing, and sometimes conflicting, scripts. And that's because they are able to input information and take on bits that for some unknown reason seem to stick in the long term. Every child, of course, reacts differently to these scripts, which is also why everyone doesn't act exactly the same at all times. Socialization, if nothing else, is an un-regulated, unpredictable human process.

Part of that process is framed by the notion of "social roles." Kids seem to pick up on this very early—who is the baby, who is the mommy, who is the daddy, who are familiars, and who are strangers. And to make those categorical assignments, children also have to know where they fit in—this is where the concept of self comes into play. After knowing self, one is then able to know who everyone else is in relation to self. And building on that comparison, kids learn what their position is as child, brother, sister, and so on. Oddly enough, children seem to take this whole system on rather easily—once they know the names, little kids love to review each person they know, repeating their roles. "You are the mommy, I am the baby." They know instinctively that adults and older siblings have power over them and that strangers are not to be trusted. Their radar for the social roles of others is actually highly developed. Although no one has researched this idea, clearly children are hard-wired to take in and accept social roles; they come equipped to place everyone in his or her place and to know who they belong to.

Psychologists say that there is constant tension during this process because it forces children to play their concept of self off others, and they learn that others have feelings and wants that sometimes are more important. "Mommy wants you to put on those shoes and it doesn't matter what you want." Soon they also realize that their desires are often in conflict with what society says they must do. "You can't hit because it is not allowed." How children react to this conflict is, of course, mediated by their own temperament and personality. Some are more passive, some more aggressive, some are easygoing or more fearful.

Children also take on an identity during socialization, one that is formed according to gender, ethnicity, race, and social class. That identity seems to be central both to a sense of self and a sense of others. Identity is, of course, intertwined with social roles—children, like adults, like to know who they are and to which group they belong. So far, there is no scientific evidence demonstrating that other primates have the same sort of identity issues. But they clearly do have a level of identity that is important. The powerful male gorilla who has high rank knows it. The female baboon who is high-ranking easily pushes others away from food and so she also knows it. And other primates clearly have a sense of belonging to a particular group. Territorial animals will defend their space quite vigorously and they know who belongs inside the lines of the group and who does not. To transfer across groups takes both courage and skill—a male baboon, for example, will befriend females of a group they want to join, thus ingratiating himself into the band.[3]

And so there are signs that a need for identity—and the resulting categories of "us" and "them" has a long evolutionary history. Children naturally identify with certain groups, genders, and such because they have a compelling need to do so. This need to have an identity is so pervasive, so critical, that it must be part of human nature. To not identify is to not belong. And so one thing we do as parents is provide the context for that identity. That context is framed, of course, by the identity we have as parents. Categorize yourself, and you'll find you have a list of the ways in which you anchor your identity, as well as the context you inevitably pass on to your child—female, working woman, white middle class, and so on. But you can also provide new facets of identity when you expose your child to new opportunities and a broader identity than your own.

In general, socialization is necessary because it allows groups of people to get along. This is part of our primate (that is, social) nature. But there may be other evolutionary forces at work as well. A small group of researchers have been trying to integrate a deeper form of evolutionary theory into thoughts on socialization.[4] They contend that beyond trying to make citizens out of kids, parents have yet another strategy—they are hoping to direct kids into finding mates, having babies, and passing on genes. Now, no one says this is a conscious plan by parents. But rather a more subtle push to be part of society, grow up, and have a family—and in doing so passing on genes. In other words, they think the process of socialization and the reason parents are so involved, so concerned, has been molded by natural selection. Kids pay attention to relationships, and how to make bonds, and they learn at home what makes a good relationship and what makes a bad one. As a result, how kids traverse their own life course can be influenced by what they see. If the bonds at home are good, they are socialized to make good bonds themselves, increasing the odds of mating and having babies—or passing on genes in the language of evolutionary theory.

Developmental psychologist Jay Belsky also thinks home life socialization can have a different effect. Belsky has proposed that children, especially girls, brought up in emotionally shaky households will reach sexual maturity earlier, thus improving their chances of getting out of the house and on their own. Such a strategy might also improve their reproductive success, since they enter adulthood earlier and presumably start having children of their own earlier.

Socialization, then, is the way a child develops from "little savage" to upright citizen. This process, however, is neither smooth nor predictable. It is also not well understood by scientists. There is the intimate influence of parents and family, the broader influence of peers and society, and the overall framework of culture. Together, these various influences provide a context for childhood, a context that clearly makes a difference—a child brought up on a rural farm in Kenya is different in most ways from a child brought up in an upper-class household in America. And just as clearly, as parents, we can choose from an array of influences to direct our children, to a certain degree, toward one path or another.

The Moral Child

Right and wrong. Good and bad. Moral and amoral. These are the opposing values of behavior, and we hope our children will grow up on the side of right, good and moral. Do we teach them how to be good, or is there some sort of basic blueprint of morality?

Morality, of course, is based on the mental ability to put oneself into the mind of another (see Chapter Five).[5] Without empathy, first of all, you cannot have a moral society. We have to "know" that harming someone hurts, "know" how the victim of wrongful behavior will feel like. Moral rules are also based on the notion that as a society we have to have some sort of structure to get along—without such rules we would be a wild horde with everyone doing whatever he or she wishes. And so people all over the world, and presumably since we humans gathered in groups, have constructed acceptable rules of behavior. But these rules only work because of the particular biological underpinnings of our particular brains allow us to be empathetic with our fellow citizens. And we expect our kids to work within this system as well.

Since the late 1950s, psychologists have utilized a basic theory for the development of morality.[6] Under this scheme, people move through levels of moral reasoning. They begin, as children, with level one, in which self-interest is the prime motivation for being good. At stage one within this level, the child acts nicely so he or she isn't punished, and then they move on to be motivated by rewards. At stage two, a person will be motivated by external rewards (that is, social approval rather than self-interest). They might act nicely so that others will like them, or because bad behavior is socially unacceptable and against the law. Eventually, people usually reach level three in which the moral system has become so ingrained that it is an abstract idea—they behave morally because it's the right thing to do. Some people, of course, never reach this third level.

Developmental psychologist William Damon has tried to figure out how kids take on the morals of adults. He feels that young children have a far "richer" sense of morals than this simple model proposes. He tests kids in the lab to see how they interact over tasks and rewards. Four children, ages four, six, or ten, for example, were asked to make beaded necklaces and then the testers handed out bits of chocolate as a reward and instructed the kids to divide up the spoils. The children turned out to be surprisingly

egalitarian and not that self-interested. They wanted to be fair—
and this in a culture that promotes self-interest above all else.[7] Little kids have also shown that they feel acts that hurt others are
much worse than acts that amount to bad manners.[8] In other
words, children probably come equipped to be morally fair toward
others; acting morally out of fear of punishment is a secondary motivation for good behavior. And that secondary motivation is
learned later.

And this makes sense. Humans are first and foremost social
animals and thus they must play by social rules. Conflict may be
inherent in a social group—there is never enough of everything to
go around—but being in a group also means you have to resolve
those conflicts.[9] Morality, as a way to get people to get along,
should therefore be grounded in how what one does affects others.[10] In that way, our moral system connects us, forms a framework for interacting. And our kids both come with the ability to
understand this very early and the mental capacity to build on that
moral foundation as they grow.

Damon also points out that some moral values are universal.
Acts like lying, theft, and bodily harm are considered wrong by all
cultures. But beyond those major negatives, ones that may be part
of the human blueprint, there are moral nuances per culture and
per social strata. Talking back to elders may be wrong in one society but not that bad in another. Cheating those in power may be
okay for the lower classes but not the upper classes. Each segment
of society, and each family, in fact, has a finer-tuned moral code.
Difference among groups is often confusing because each segment
believes they have the best, finest, most righteous moral code. And
so a system that evolved to help humans get along in a complex so-

ciety takes on a political tone. And that's why instructing our kids about what is right and what is wrong is often so confusing.

Children have the basics and then they learn the rest by experience and instruction. What parents tell them, and how parents act, is key. Since moral behavior begins so early, and since kids are able to absorb so much early on, the moral systems become part of who we are. Researchers like Damon point out that some people have a moral code, but not everyone acts on that code—just about everyone knows that victims of a disaster are in trouble and it's morally wrong not to help them, but only a subset of people actually volunteer. Those people, researchers find, have integrated their moral code into their very identity.[11] For whatever reason, their very sense of self is entwined with doing the right thing. They are also people who have grown up in a community where the moral rules are consistent.

And so this is yet another job for family and community—to consistently tell children about what is right and what is wrong, to play on their innate ability to feel what others feel. Again, this is a process, not a one-shot deal, and there is a lot of variation in the way kids hear what we say and do what we tell them.

Socialization in Other Cultures

All parents hope to socialize their children into polite society; one of the more compelling parenting goals is to guide children into adulthood. But how parents do this, and the very social goals they embrace, vary widely across the globe. Anthropologists are especially interested in how parents do this, and they have tried to

Childhood in Western culture is considered a time of freedom, fun, and learning. *Dede Hatch*

ABOVE Only recently has there been a focus on childhood as a special time with toys, clothing, furniture, and entertainment designed especially for children.

Kent Loeffler

BELOW Children in other cultures work hard and contribute to the family. These Mayan children haul water, work in the fields, and care for other children.

Karen Kramer

LEFT Most child care around the world today is done by older children, which allows parents to work. *R.C. Kirkpatrick*

BELOW Childhood as a life cycle stage is unique to humans. Other primates, like these macaque monkeys, move quickly from infancy to adolescence and then into adulthood. *M. F. Small*

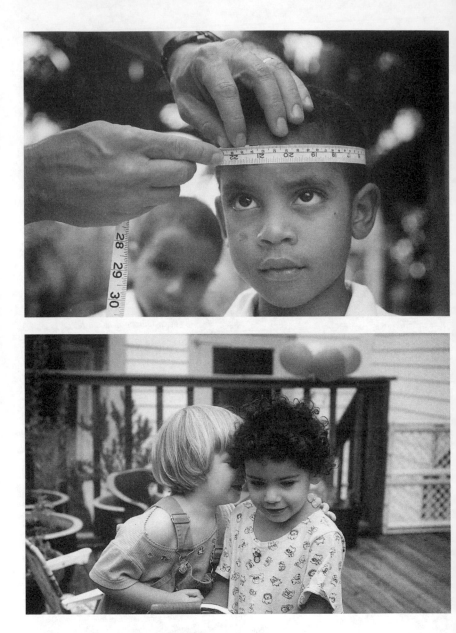

ABOVE One of the main features of childhood is growth. *Lynn Johnson*

BELOW Children are biologically predisposed to acquire language. That process is also influenced by family conversation, time with peers, and culture. *M. F. Small*

ABOVE Children also learn in formal ways through instruction at school and home. *Dede Hatch*

BELOW Mark Flinn studies the effect of family trauma on children in a rural village in Dominica. *Lynn Johnson*

ABOVE In some societies, parents favor one sex over another. Among the Mokodogo, girls are treated better than boys because girls are more likely to marry up in status. *Beth L. Leech*

BELOW We might begin to question the Western ideal of endless consumer goods for children. Do such goods really make more successful, happier adults? *M. F. Small*

ABOVE Children have always found ways to make toys and have a good time. These Tanzanian children have fashioned a bicycle out of wood.

M. F. Small

RIGHT Our job as parents, family, community members, and a species is to provide a loving and interesting environment for the smallest members of our kind.

Harry Littell

make sense of the paths of socialization. One of the major contributors to this field is Robert LeVine of Harvard University. LeVine and his wife, Sarah LeVine, have worked with the Gusii people of western Kenya for over forty years, comparing Gusii parents and kids to the Western cultural model. Through this work, LeVine has developed a general model for understanding broad goals of socialization that can be applied to various societies. These goals, LeVine says, are not so much philosophical ideals as reflections of very real survival strategies. Socialization styles, he believes, are molded by how critically the life and health of their children are threatened. For the Gusii, and many other third world people, infant mortality is high, sometimes as much as 50 percent, and parents naturally mold their parenting to stave off infant death. Gusii babies, for example, are held all the time and never, ever, left alone. In the West, where infant mortality is much lower, we are less vigilant and have more time to concentrate on teaching our babies.[12] At a fundamental level, then, parents want their small infants to survive, but this is more an issue in some cultures than others. Next, once the threat of death has decreased somewhat during childhood, all parents want their kids to be trained, taught, and able to fend for themselves. And when all that is achieved, parents hope to foster other cultural values that will help a child be a success in that particular culture.[13] LeVine then combines these three stages and comes up with two broad patterns for explaining types of socialization across human groups. When infant mortality is high, parents will be most concerned with the health and survival of their infants during the early stages. These babies will be held all the time, watched, and coddled. They will not concentrate on learning and training, but have intense physical relationships with their small children. And in societies where infant mortality is low, parents will be less compelled to worry about health and survival and more free to focus on skills that may serve kids in the future. Once the child's survival is assured (that is, once they are past the first year or so), parents focus on training the child for their future, that is education and such. The Gusii, of course, are more oriented toward the first pattern—babies are held at all times, protected, fed on cue, but they do not receive lessons or a lot of chat. American babies, of course, are less physically vulnerable because of their relatively affluent culture and better health care, and so American parents have extended the learning period way into infancy because they can afford to do so. By and large, LeVine's dichotomous system works; it explains broad patterns of socialization across cultures. It underscores why babies in third world cultures seem so coddled to Westerners, and why third world parents are so amazed that Western parents encourage their small children to walk and talk and be independent. But within the broad theory that LeVine presents are variations on those two socialization scripts that have additional roots in the ecology, subsistence patterns, future goals, and traditions of various cultures.

You can't find a culture more different from Western culture than the Mbuti pygmies of the Ituri Forest, Zaire, Central Africa. These smaller than average people are forest hunters and gatherers; even today, many Mbuti still carry on in traditional ways. Years ago, anthropologist Colin Turnbull spent time living with and documented Mbuti ways.[14] Although this ethnographic work is several decades old, it stands as a model of how the Mbuti live, and luckily, Turnbull wasn't exclusive in his observations. In fact, he was interested in all the life cycle stages, describing in papers and books what it means to grow up Mbuti.

As a people, the Mbuti are part of the forest—they love the forest and respect it. And they are a nonaggressive, nonviolent people who believe in sharing and connection. Child care is shared, and everyone looks out for every kid. In fact, the kinship naming system does not follow strict biological lines—children learn early that names for kin such as grandmother and grandfather relate to those who care for children, even nonblood relatives. Little ones also learn that there are age categories that matter—other kids, youths, adults, and elders—and that one must interact with others in age-appropriate ways.

By the age of two, Mbuti children join other kids at a play area called the *bopi.* Here they will have same-age playmates and also interact with kids of other ages. Here also is where they first encounter aggression, and they learn that such aggression and competition is not tolerated. The best way to avoid conflict, these children learn, is to be mobile—just walk away and be somewhere else. And if all else fails, laugh. Turnbull says that laughter is "the Mbutis' prime weapon against conflict, aggression, and violence."[15]

And so the *bopi* becomes a major arena for socialization—this is where they interact with peers, where they fight and avoid fights, where they take on kinship and sex roles. Here they imitate domestic chores and use their imagination and invent games as well. Here they settle disputes and exercise their interpersonal verbal skills; children are immersed in the use of language as a way to get along. And they share everything with those of the same age;

at this point, there is no division by gender. It's a noisy, happy place where children can explore themselves and others. "Laughter, jokes, and ridicule are vital elements in Mbuti life," writes Turnbull, and kids use all three.

This time before puberty, before they get initiated into adulthood, is one of freedom and play. But the play has meaning; they must learn to avoid conflict, get along, use language to resolve disputes and tell stories. And they must absorb the various ties among group members while building their own lifelong ties as they interact with other kids on the *bopi*. Socialization is not just the job of parents or the community, but of the collective group of children as well; they teach each other. The values of Mbuti life— connection, nonviolence, sharing—are imparted early and reinforced daily by all members. This is a collective endeavor.

This description of Mbuti childhood contrasts sharply with how children are socialized on the island of Tonga, half a world away in the South Pacific. Anthropologist Helen Morton spent several years living on Tonga—she also married a Tongan and had a child there. Years later she brought her son back to the island for more field work.[16] Morton was struck with the negative and positive sides of Tongan parenting, a conflict that was hard for her Western mind to resolve. Adults seem to both love children and yet speak ill of them; they say children are gifts that enrich your life and also call them lazy, bad, and tiring. They beat children when they are bad, and then hug them.

Life on Tonga echoes that of much of the semideveloped world. There are small garden plots that provide some food and these plots are usually tended by women and men. Adults also work in other arenas as taxi drivers, teachers, or in offices. Children go to school, but the resources at these schools are scarce. Women are in charge of child care; until the age of two, babies stay with their mothers. Caretaking for infants echoes that of most people around the world (except the West)—babies are carried all of the time by someone, they are included in all adult social activities, they sleep with mother, breast-feeding is the norm, relatives help out with caretaking.

But when these favored infants can walk and talk, they enter into the next stage of life, childhood, which is less than idyllic. Adults believe that the goal of children is to become *poto,* which means "clever, socially competent, and capable."[17] They recognize that children are born with certain inherited dispositions, but that they can also be molded; on Tonga, they emphasize the shaping of a child, rather than its innate disposition. Children are considered naturally naughty, or mischievous, and the parental goal is to make them obey. Morton found that parents constantly talked of their children as "foolish, naughty, impulsive, and difficult to look after."[18] And yet parents seem to think these qualities are natural and normal, expected; they were not noted as complaints. Parents see girls as generally nicer than boys. Socialization, Morton found, was aimed to making kids "good" (that is, transforming these naturally mischievous creatures into well-behaved adults).

Good behavior is motivated by invoking one's reputation—if a child is bad, he or she will shame himself or herself and the family. Children must learn to assess a situation and then act in a way that is "right." Moreover, children are as invested in the process as adults. Morton asked 230 teenagers what were the most important things they were taught as children. Topping the list were proper behavior, religion, and obedience, all important to adult cultural identity. Morton feels these values are invoked when parents emphasize that behavior and its consequences, rather than what the child feels, are what are important. Tongans don't care how the children feel, only that they obey.

Children on Tonga are expected to be respectful and obey adults. As a sign of respect, they are often silent around adults, who are, by definition, individuals of higher status. Freedom and independence, values so important in the West, are treated with ambivalence. Kids are not encouraged to do things on their own, and yet the children also somehow learn that independence is a good thing. Somewhere in the mix of a strict status hierarchy, family obligations, and parental authority, kids are also encouraged to develop a sense of autonomy.

Tongan playgroups are of mixed ages and sex, and many of the play partners are relatives. Kids' games are often rough—there's lots of hitting and pushing and general aggression and parents usually don't intervene. In fact, adults rarely play with kids, thinking this is a waste of time. Morton describes the spheres of children and adults as rather separate, even when the household is together—children will be at one end of the house playing, while parents are at the other end talking. When adults do play with kids, there's lots of teasing and smacking and children end up crying—it's a rough game and little children can't keep up.

In general, Tongan children receive a lot of physical punishment compared to Western standards—and an extreme amount compared to Mbuti kids. They are hit by hand, stick, belt, broom, whatever is at hand. They are also handled roughly, pushed and pulled by parents and older playmates. And if the child cries or makes a fuss, the punishment continues—soon they learn to control their emotions as well as their behavior. This way, self-control is fostered.

Tongan parents, and children when they grow up, say this kind of physical punishment is a part of loving. They believe it is an essential part of socialization, a necessary way of molding naturally mischievous, uncontrolled young ones. Sometimes such punishment borders on abuse, as it does in all cultures in which it is acceptable to physically harm children. Lately, the Tongans themselves have been looking into the issue, wondering if physical punishment is really necessary, even if it is traditional.

The point is that every culture, every subgroup, has goals that are embraced by the adult members. These goals, these ways of being, are passed along by parents and society as a whole. Some of the ways we steer kids to these goals are subtle—"We just don't do it that way." Others are not so subtle—"If you do that, I will punish you." Children are designed to watch, absorb, and conform. Interesting enough, children rarely protest when these goals are imposed on them—in fact, kids try very hard to be like everyone else, especially adults. Without question, we all socialize to our own culture, ethnicity, class, religion, and gender. This is our identity, this is who we are. And as parents, we provide the means to this socialization process. Harder to keep in mind is that this process is flexible, changeable, and not some set of rules set in stone that must be followed. Just as cultures change over time, so do the social rules.

Discipline

All kids act up. Regardless of the child, regardless of the parents, regardless of the culture, at some point even the most well-behaved child does something unacceptable. And as part of his or her socialization, that behavior must be "dealt with." Of course, there are many ways to deal with bad behavior, and most parents flounder around trying to figure out how to stop hitting, grabbing, pushing, and the like. These attempts are based on some sort of parenting philosophy, a philosophy that is part of a larger parental script, which in turn is anchored in culture and history.

First of all, every culture and every set of parents within the culture has a particular idea of the nature of children. The Western view has been influenced by the Greeks and the Romans, who believed that children were unformed, moldable, and rather wild. Kids, according to Western tradition, were in need of control.[19] And so, strong discipline was the order of the day in ancient Greek and Roman times. Layered on top of that Greek and Roman view is the approach of the Puritans, who felt that children were born into this world with original sin and they had to be broken and cleansed with discipline.[20] The Puritans felt that developing moral character was of high importance and that the overall role of parents was to both instruct and to discipline. Add to this Puritan ethic a dash of John Locke's view that children are free spirits that should be allowed to develop at will, with only rational explanations as a guide. Locke, an influential philosopher of the time, felt that a combination of praise and shame would do the trick. And then follow Locke with Rousseau's influential notion that children are nature's gifts that should not be punished at all. The result is the confusing picture presented to American parents of how children are and what they need in terms of discipline—they are either free spirits that should roam free or unruly beings in need of order. There is no consensus on the nature of the child in the West—go to any playground and interview any ten parents and you will likely get ten different philosophies.

Recently, Western parents have also been influenced by current work on genetics and the role genes might play in human behavior. Educated parents are also influenced by the glut of scientific studies and advice books; they look to "experts" to tell them how to stop this or that behavior. Some parents take the Puritan road and see their child as ruffians in need of strict rules. Others may think of childhood as a carefree time of fun and play and are less likely to set limits lest such rules destroy this perceived childhood nirvana. When my niece and nephew were very young, I remember my sister telling me, "I never want anyone to say the word 'no' to my children. I want them to think anything is possible." Other parents take the opposite tack. I have friends who believe in firm rules, limits, expectations, and freely use the word "no" with their kids. In both cases, consistency on the parents' part is seen as critical.

Today American parents also believe in the notion of "self-control" or "self-regulation," which also has religious roots—kids should "choose," on their own, to be good, which of course is a moral expectation. They should be forming their own moral code, one that matches their parents and is in accord with society. As developmental psychologist Ellen Peisner, who has written about the history of discipline, writes, "Such a view contains an implicit assumption that children play an active role in their own development."[21] In other words, expecting kids to take on the moral system of adults assumes they will internalize what is external, what they have been told over and over, and become morally like everyone else in that particular society.

In general, the belief systems of each culture about the nature of childhood directs how discipline is meted out. Individual parents, and individual children, work within that cultural model and come up with a system of expectations, rules, and standard interactions. All parents, of course, are convinced that their system is "right," both in its moral stance and how they go about disciplining children. It's harder to step back and look at other parents, and other cultures, and realize that there may be other views of childhood, other ways to make model citizens.

No one is sure exactly how discipline is supposed to work, if it works at all. Although the word "discipline" has a negative connotation, there are both positive and negative forms.[22] For example, screaming at a child is the obvious negative form. The tone of voice of the parent is unhappy, his or her face is contorted in disapproval, and the child clearly knows this. Distracting a child, a strategy that does not present an unhappy tone of voice or facial expression, is an example of the more positive form. Both aim to correct behavior, or turn it in another direction. Research on American kids shows that the negative form doesn't really work—negative punishment, such as slapping, spanking, or yelling at a child, only begets more bad behavior.[23] In these interactions, it appears, children learn that their behavior elicits response, attention, and drives parents out of control. This can be rather exciting for the child, and therefore reinforcingly positive from the kid's point of view. In the worst form of negative punishment, bodily harm, such action might subdue a child, but it also scars them physically and psychologically for life; child abuse can be handed down through generations, as those who were abused then tend to abuse their own children.

Positive "punishment" (that is, ignoring the behavior or distracting the child and then rewarding good behavior) seems to have better results. These nonpunitive strategies also include talking to the child and explaining why a behavior is unacceptable— "Don't hit because it's not nice, you don't like it when people hit you. Do you see Mommy hitting? Daddy hitting? Then you don't hit." This method is favored by middle- and upper-class Americans, who in general ascribe to conversation with their children. These parents also believe that they have the power to mold their children, that the kids will eventually "get it" if the parents just keep repeating the explanations over and over. Lengthy explanations are less frequent among those who are less affluent, and in most other cultures where respect for authority is a primary goal for parents. Such explanations, to them, seem frivolous and unnecessary.[24] Lengthy explanations aren't needed, because these children are expected to do what they are told.

The Western discipline pattern in general is rather confusing because it is not consistent across-the-board.[25] Children are not told to be obedient in all things. Parents want them to be independent and free-minded at times but also obedient. It just doesn't work that way. And so they pick and choose—you can't climb the stairs, but look how great it is you can climb over the sofa—and this makes for constant monitoring, policing, and deciding which behaviors need discipline, so the message is not particularly clear to children. In other cultures, where obedience is the general rule, there is no decision, a mulling things over—kids must do everything they are told, keep quiet, and obey.

In Western culture, most parents try lots of parenting techniques. Their rate of success depends on the personality and temperament of the child, the developmental age of the child, the particular parental script, and the nature of the family system. It also depends on the perception of the child—having Mommy chase you when you are bad might seem a reward to some. Each parent or caretaker has a different style or finds different behaviors more annoying; the rules at day care are probably different from those at home, and Mommy and Daddy themselves might have opposing ideas as well. Most parents alter their strategies when they don't work and they try something else.

Across cultures, parents deal with bad behavior in all sorts of ways as well. Above I described intense physical punishment doled out by parents and others on the island of Tonga. Hitting a child, pushing him around, is normal and expected fare on that island and on many islands in the Pacific. Children don't fight back, and they soon learn not to even cry, since that is punished as well. What makes this scenario so fascinating for scientists is that babies are indulged compared with Western standards—they are held and hugged all the time and watched intently by everybody. And so children move from a social arena in which they are the coddled centers of attention to a toddlerhood in which they are vulnerable to physical punishment.

Discipline, it seems, is one of the more flexible and dynamic child-hood events. And as in many of the human endeavors, it shows a continuum, from the lack of any sort of punishment in some hunters and gatherers, such as the San or the Mbuti; through Western standards of little punishment; to the Pacific, where corporal punishment and ridicule is the norm. It's important to realize that all of this is culturally relative—every group's goals form the rules they apply. At the same time, there are standards of behavior toward children that should be universal. They are our most vulnerable citizens. Yes, they need to be socialized and each adult plays a part in the process, but no one has the right to harm a child, not even a well-intended parent. Punishment is not the same as discipline. Pain is not a way to show love and attachment. And these values are not culturally laden values, they are human rights.

CHAPTER SEVEN

Girls and Boys

In 1993, anthropologist Amy Parish decided to run a gender experiment. She knew from an amniocentesis that she was about to give birth to a son, but she hadn't shared the information with anyone but the baby's father. One day Parish was about to tell her brother the exciting news—a nephew on the way!—when her brother cut the conversation short. "I don't want to know the sex of the baby," he said, "because it shouldn't matter."

Stopped in her tracks, Parish started thinking about her brother's view, and she realized that it really *shouldn't* matter. What difference does it really make if the baby is a boy or girl? she ruminated. The anthropologist in her was intrigued, and the social scientist in her wanted to conduct a test and make a point. And so Parish and her partner, Volker Sommer, decided to keep the information about the baby's sex to themselves, even after their son

Kahlind's birth. When showing off their newborn, they made no reference to his sex, using neutral pronouns when they had to say something. Kahlind became "it," rather than "he."

"It was really hard to do," remembers Parish seven years later. "We are so used to making references as male or female, this is so much part of how we talk and a lesson in how we use these terms. So it became difficult."

The reaction from friends was also startling, says Parish. "People would ask if he was a boy or a girl and I would refuse to answer, and they got very upset." Some, even good friends, accused the parents of "withholding information." Others suggested something more damaging could happen. When denied the baby's sex, people might think there was something wrong, perhaps a sex chromosomal defect that had rendered the baby neither male nor female—and would she want the baby to carry that mark? More amusing, their nonsex stand sent the whole present giving ritual into a tizzy. "What can we give the baby if we don't know if it's a boy or girl?" many asked. Some even blackmailed Parish and Sommer, saying they refused to give a gift until they knew Kahlind's sex.

The experiment lasted a few weeks and then the parents gave in. "All the begging to know," says Parish, "became tiring." And not using pronouns when referring to the baby also got old in public. Kahlind was a boy and so he took on that gender, and everyone around Parish and Sommer, and their son, calmed down.

What is it about sex, the categories of male and female, that is so important to humans that we just have to know? Of all the attributes that we might use to categorize our own kind—race, height, weight, religion, ethnicity, eye color, mouth shape—sex is the one that is applied first and used most consistently by ourselves and others as a marker of identity. Sex, it seems, is paramount to human identity; first you are human and then you are either male or female. As such, one's sex and its corresponding gender take on special significance when considering how kids are socialized and become members of a culture.

Babies have no gender. Yes, they have different sex chromosomes and different genitalia, and therefore are of a certain sex, but other than that, they are just baby humans. Gender is not so much a characteristic as a process, the path of maleness or femaleness that one travels; it is defined not by chromosomes or genitals but by thought, feelings, behavior, and outward appearance.

Knowing one's gender, and the gender of others, is part of the ever-important subject of identity; knowing if you are female or male is a major part of knowing who you are. Although volumes have been written about how genderization—which is often a polarizing exercise—happens in Western culture and other cultures, but no one has yet figured out *why* it is so important to us to belong to one gender or the other. We start out with different genitalia, but that's about all. Yet from the minute of birth, we place pink hats or blue hats on our kids, give them dresses with ruffles or jeans and T-shirts, grow their hair long or cut it off, and in just about every way push our infants and children into the appropriate category.

Is There a Biology of Gender?

Are there biological differences between boys and girls? Of course there are. Take the standard human infant blueprint and check it out. One has folds between the legs and a vagina, the other has a penis. And if we took blood from these specimens we would see that the twenty-third pair of chromosomes of one, the female, were two big strands of DNA (two X chromosomes), while for the male, the twenty-third pair is comprised of one large strand and one small strand of DNA (one X and one Y). These chromosomal differences set in motion a different recipe for a hormonal mix that will eventually, at sexual maturity, exaggerate certain body features, making the two sexes easier to distinguish; females will get breasts and wider hips, males will grow facial hair. And these changes are there to facilitate the mating process. Those with the breasts also have ovaries that make eggs, while those with the facial hair have testes that make sperm. A meeting of the two is necessary to make another human and thus pass on genes.

We are a sexually reproducing species and therefore we have two sexes that mate to create more of their kind. Many organisms on Earth don't reproduce this way—they clone themselves. We belong to the group of animals that combines DNA to make offspring. This strategy, scientists believe, evolved because offspring with a combination of two parental genes might do better in a dangerous and ever-changing world than a species that simply makes exact copies of each individual.[1] In a sense, it's an arms race. Diseases and pathogens are always mutating and taking over organisms. The only defense is a good immune system. But the diseases are mutating faster than their hosts, and so parents who combine their genes and produce an offspring with a mix and match of genes, thereby producing a more resistant immune system in the next generation, will have a better chance. Sexual reproduction, then, evolved to make better offspring in changing environments, more resistant and able kids.

And so we have two sexes so that we can have sex, so that we can recombine our DNA, but no one is sure exactly what it means for the organisms themselves to be one sex or the other.

During human infancy and early childhood, there are developmental differences among children, but few of them can be related to sex. There is some evidence that males reach various developmental stages sometimes behind girls, but these differences are not so regular that it happens in every case—often boys will speed past girls, or the differences in timing are so slight as to be meaningless. There is also some evidence for studies in Western culture that when girls begin to acquire language, they use it more adeptly in the social sense than boys do.[2] But the language studies are often confounding and in the end, the sexes generally talk the same; there is probably more variation among children than between the sexes.

No one is sure about the biological underpinnings of differences in behavior. We do know that hormones influence the feelings of maleness or femaleness, and those feelings are inextricably entwined with what we do. We know this because some people are born with odd chromosomal compliments and hormonal conditions that alter the sexual organs and children's behavior. For example, children can be born with an X and Y chromosome (that is, their sex chromosomes indicate they are male) but be insensitive to the dictates of testosterone because of a faulty X chromosome (a condition called *androgen insensitivity syndrome*). These children are chromosomally male but physiologically more female—they have a mix and match of reproductive organs, some male and some female parts, and no chance of reproducing themselves.[3] Until very recently, removing any male parts, such as internal testicles, soon after birth was the norm. The female parts were later enhanced—for example, the vagina, which tends to be short, was lengthened. The bodies of these children have basically defaulted, with surgical help, to the female pattern. They don't respond to testosterone and are therefore biologically female. More intriguing, women with this syndrome reportedly "feel" female and "act" female, regardless of their Y chromosome.

This syndrome is one of many that can result in individuals with ambiguous sex, ambiguous gender, and ambiguous genderized behavior. We are biological systems, and fetal development is vulnerable to all sorts of detours. Parents sometimes have to make difficult decisions about how to deal with a baby that is biologically one way, but a way that is not acceptable in a sexually pluralistic society. In fact, behavior is such a continuum that the very way we define male or female feelings and acts is superficial. The behavior according to gender, then, is a slippery slope.

Some have suggested that there must be differences in the brain and underlying neurological systems of males and females, that we are "wired" differently, as opposed to just socialized differently. Indeed, researchers have found that there may be sex differences in such things as inhibition and self-control, although these studies have only been conducted in Western culture. If these differences can be upheld, they may be related to biological differences in the brain, specifically in the developmental rate of the prefrontal lobe.[4] But so far, research on brain differences by sex in children, as well as adults, is in its infancy, and the results thus far have been contradictory and unclear, suggesting there may be only slight, or biologically insignificant, differences. It's more interesting to note, I think, that millions of dollars of research money have been spent searching for these differences in mental abilities and brain function. Our scientifically oriented culture, it seems, believes one of the pressing questions about humans is the possibility that men and women might have different brains. Why is this so important to us, I wonder?

Gender is related to sex, and sex is related to chromosomes and hormones, but the interplay between them is highly flexible. How behavior intersects with those chromosomes and hormones is a murky soup of biology, experience, and the perspective of parents and society. What does it really mean to be a girl child or a boy child? Do boys and girls think differently, act differently, have different emotions?

Behaving Like a Girl or a Boy

Children up to the age of four don't have the cognitive power to really understand what it means to be one sex or another; their gender identification is rather superficial. They can't identify the sex of dolls with male or female genitalia, and they often mix up their own sex as well as that of others; gender has nothing to do with physicality for them.[5] Instead, they label someone male or female based on hair or clothing, or what Mommy or Daddy has said. And until they are about four years old, gender is a fluid concept to young children—they might call themselves a boy today and a girl tomorrow. By the time they are four years old, however, they realize that gender, and their sex, is fixed, a concept called "gender constancy" by child development researchers.[6] From that point on, they have rather rigid ideas of the parameters of "correct" behavior for each sex and don't like it when other kids or adults cross the line; later in childhood, their ideas soften and they don't care as much when girls act "like boys," for example.[7]

A volume of research has attempted to document differences in behavior among small children, and these studies echo what most parents see at home. Boys seem to be more active, engage in more rough-and-tumble play and are more aggressive than little girls. But these differences don't appear until kids are over two years of age, and they are highly dependent on the context of the study. For example, psychologist Eleanor Maccoby, who has made a life's work of looking at gender differences in kids, found that given the opportunity, and free of interference from boys, girls are just as active as boys.[8] Girls play hard outdoors, but they are much less active indoors, and so the impression that parents and teachers have is moderated by where they watch kids play. And when alone, which might be the best predictor of some sort of natural, biological difference in activity level between boys and girls, kids act the same. "When children are playing alone," writes Maccoby, "sex differences in activity level are minimal."[9]

But everything changes, Maccoby and others say, when children get together with their peers. That's when real sex differences appear. When preschool boys hang out together, they feed on each other and their activity level goes wild. Is this a biological difference? Between the ages of two and four, boys have a slightly higher metabolic rate than girls, but left to their own devices, they show no higher energy levels—metabolic rate is not directly related to activity level. Also, boys tend to be less physically mature than girls of the same age, and this might account for why girls seem to be less active; with maturity, metabolic rate slows down. But Maccoby maintains that it's the social context, the interacting with peers, that gets boys going, rather than innate biological differences at the level of the individual.

Society also unconsciously molds, or reinforces, what are slight differences between boys and girls. Adults have ideas about how kids "should" act, according to gender, and their expectations both color their views of child behavior and at the same time reinforce certain roles. Boys are most often viewed as uncontrollable and talked about by adults in a negative light. Girls, on the other hand, are considered to be more cooperative and less aggressive. When deviations from these roles occur, parents and others tend to ignore what they see. Children, of course, quickly learn how to act appropriately. They do so for approval and to fit in with their peers.

The one major difference in behavior that researchers have documented for groups of girls and boys is that over three years of age, children like other children of the same gender. They all play pretty much the same way, at the same interactive level, but boys prefer to play with boys and girls prefer to play with girls.[10] This preference lasts through the preschool years and is seen in non-Western cultures as well; same-sex groups in early childhood are a human universal.[11] Presumably, kids are drawn to their own kind because they play the same way—girls know the rules of girl play and boys follow a familiar agenda as well. And so each sex tends to group together simply because of familiarity. Boys and girls also talk a bit differently. Boys talk more about status—who is in charge, who can win, who is bigger—while girls speak more often of social connections; they are interested in who is friends with whom, not who is winning. And so each group knows how to interact more easily with those of the same gender, and they prefer to do so. Interestingly enough, young preschool children of the same gender recognize each other easily, even when dressed the same. In classic experiments where unfamiliar children of both sexes are put in a room together, dressed in a gender-neutral clothing, boys still find and prefer other boys and girls find the girls.[12] They seem to cue in on hairstyles, voice, verbal nuances, gestures, or behavior—subtle cues that they go beyond mere skirts and pants.

Parents, teachers, and society at large reinforce same-sex gender segregation. In cultures where children work, for example, girls are given domestic chores, while boys are sent outside to herd cattle, both following in the footsteps of the gender-appropriate parent. As a result, these children end up working, playing, and hanging around with their own sex. In the West, we also do this when we segregate sports and other activities by gender. And we constantly tell our little ones that they are boys or girls and tend to dress them in ways that will identify them as the "right" sex.

At the same time, research on how *parents* treat their kids shows that there are few if any differences by gender in Western culture, and when they do appear, the differences are minimal. Parents don't give either sex more attention, for example. Parents do like it when their kids play in gender-appropriate ways, when girls play with dolls and boys play with trucks (although parents are more forgiving when girls cross this play gender line). One difference that does stand out is how parents treat emotional issues—they talk more with girls about these things and expect boys to repress their emotions.

Stronger sanctions against crossing gender lines seem to come at a higher, social level. At home, in most families nobody cares that much whether or not you act appropriate to your sex, but in public, it seems to matter a good deal more. In fact, Maccoby believes that in the West, childhood culture is much more segregated by gender than adult culture is. As adults, women don't dress primarily in pink and men don't dress in blue, for example. Men and women cross the gender lines all the time at work and at home. Perhaps there is an evolutionary strategy at work here. It may be that culture presses gender more strongly on the young because soon they will be adolescents, and gender role identification becomes reproductively paramount.

Since gender identification is something that is intimately incorporated into human language and social interaction, it is no surprise that gender roles and the move toward identifying with one gender are quickly integrated into a child's worldview. Back in the 1960s, Lawrence Kohlberg suggested that such typing is just a product of a general tendency for children to categorize. But the roots might lie even deeper; such identification may have an evolutionary basis—knowing what sex you are and what the other sex is surely must be useful in adult mating. If you can't ID the opposite sex, how can you find someone to mate with and pass on genes? Other animals seem to find each other easily, but they may be going on hard-wired cues of looks or odors that make identification easy. Categorizing males and females and acting on that knowledge is one of the basics of biology we share with all sexually reproducing animals. And many species have elaborated on that theme over generations as the mating process has provoked anatomical and behavioral differences between the sexes. Male lions have manes because they fight with each other for the right to mate the opposite sex and those manes protect them from fatal injuries; female chimpanzees sport pink swellings during ovulation to attract males; male songbirds have beautiful voices to sing and attract females. Humans have used their large brains to take this "extra" layer that separates males and females beyond mere chromosomes even further.[13] But humans seem to enjoy taking genderization to its limit. No one knows why we have elaborated gender so extremely, but we have. This flourishing of gender, this concern for maleness and femaleness, seems to be an essential part of being human.

Girls and Boys Across Cultures

In the 1950s, a group of anthropologists set out on an ambitious project—they wanted to compare childhood across cultures. And so they set up six different ethnographic projects across the globe and instructed field-workers to gather information about the lives of children.[14] Although this information is now fifty years old and dated, it stands as the best cross-cultural comparative information we have about children. In the 1960s, '70s, and '80s, studies of children in other cultures were added to this data resource, extending the information to twelve cultures and allowing researchers to ask all sorts of questions about the world of children. In the late 1980s, anthropologists Beatrice Whiting and Carolyn Pope Edwards used this resource to look at how kids are socialized, and especially how various settings direct gender differences. The type of home ranged from small villages to cities, and the subsistence level ranged from individual farms to industrial economies. Although half of the sample came from African communities, India, the Philippines, the United States, and Mexico were also represented. They focused on kids ages two to ten, the time when identity and sex roles are absorbed by children.

Whiting and Edwards found that mothers, who in most countries do most or all of the child care, are the primary agents of gender typing and the division between boys and girls. "The power of mothers to assign girls and boys to different settings may be the single most important factor in shaping gender-specific behaviors in childhood," Whiting and Pope write.[15] And this division is greatest, of course, in societies where there is a strong dichotomy between adult men and women, where the adult roles are separate and their lives run on different tracks. In such societies, girls are trained earlier to contribute to the household, expected to care for young children, and are assigned domestic chores at an early age. How much little girls have to do seems to be related to maternal workload; when Mother works hard carrying water, working in the fields and such, her daughters are required to chip in. But the system is flexible; if women don't have the appropriately sexed children for particular tasks, they adapt—boys can carry babies and girls can herd sheep. Still, many boys have it easier in early childhood. Mothers try to control their young sons, but boys tend to ignore them, presumably as part of their attempt to dissociate themselves from the domestic scene and move on to the sphere of men. Even when they are assigned "female" tasks, they seem to do it a way that distinguishes their work from "girl" work. More significantly, girls are pressured early on to be responsible and socially adept, while boys are generally more free.

Edwards also found that sex segregation is the "grand rule" across cultures once kids reach age six.[16] In a survey of eleven diverse cultures, she found that young girls, from, say, the age of three on up, spend much of their time doing chores such as child care and housework, while young males of the same age seem to have more time to play. These boys soon disengage from the day-to-day workings of the household and are off on their own or with other boys. Meanwhile, girls tend to do the babysitting for smaller siblings. And so sex segregation in other cultures is not so much a choice of kids, or some ideological script of parents, but a matter of work. Although all young children are attracted to babies, it is the girls who are required to stay at home and are required to perform the actual care. Edwards feels they are more comfortable with her nurturing style than the more distant model that fathers provide. In that way, both sexes are socialized through generations to repeat the patterns of adults, to the point where it looks and feels "natural" to everyone.

Some cultures start gender differentiation early. Indian and Mexican baby girls have pierced ears; toddler hairstyles and clothing also differ by sex. Other cultures are less interested in these accoutrements. In any case, where the weather is warm and little kids don't wear anything below the waist, their sexual organs and their sex are obvious.

All kids see that in almost every culture, and this includes the West, men are more highly valued. Such power underscores the ultimate meaning of gender differences. "There are countless acts witnessed by children that symbolize the differential power of men and women," comment Whiting and Edwards.[17] Women cook and men are served their food; women wash, men wear those clothes; women till fields and men herd the more valuable cattle; women stop child care and get dinner when Dad comes home. The message is clear about the differences between the sexes. And it becomes even more clear as kids reach adolescence and various initiation rites elevate boys and ignore girls. Boys become men with status, power, and goods, while girls become women who are traded off in marriage.

Examples from other cultures can be enlightening. Too often, we look only at those who are just like ourselves, and what we see becomes only what is acceptable. Although all human children are biologically male and female, and men and women in all cultures take on male and female gender roles, the way that cultures socialize their citizens differs. Looking at some examples of other cultures can not only open our minds to other ways, such an exercise can make us look at our own process of genderization in a new way. Such self-examination can also lead to fruitful change.

The village of Khalapur, Uttar Pradesh, India, lies in a fertile plain in the shadow of the Himalayas. It is a jumbled hodgepodge of a village, a maze of alleyways, mud houses, and crowded neighborhoods. There are complex rules of behavior here, bounding religion, kinship, and caste restrictions that guide behavior.[18]

Parents believe that children are formed when they arrive and that there is little you can teach them; training is not important.

And so until a child can talk, no one bothers to teach them anything. Once they speak, young children are still thought to be unable to do much beyond carry out the most simple commands. Learning at this age, everyone believes, occurs by observation and imitation, not direction.

All little children of the Rajput clan wear the same clothes—a shirt and no diapers or underpants, which facilitates learning how to urinate and defecate down the appropriate drain at the edge of the yard. But when the weather turns cold, boys are bundled into padded coats, while girls are wrapped in an adult sari or jacket. Both sexes wear their hair short, in the Hindu style, although girls might have a braid that they attach. Girls also sport bracelets and an anklet, unlike boys.

Adult life in Khalapur is strongly segregated by sex, but this is less true for young children, who interact with kids of both sexes. Mothers prefer that their children play in groups rather than alone. As they grow older, the children, like kids the world over, prefer their own sex because they play the same sort of games. Although there are few toys around, children still play at adult roles; girls play house by making mud pies, while boys make pretend bows and arrows or play at farming.

Unlike many cultures in which kids are expected to work, the children of Khalapur are more free to play. They might run a few errands or wash dishes, but these tasks are occasional. In fact, girls receive a special dispensation. Mothers tell their daughters that when they grow up, they will have to work hard in their husbands' houses, and so they should have fun now. Rajput mothers continue to dress, bathe, and serve children until they are in grammar school—self-reliance is not a quality they look for and neither is responsibility. Mothers talk of obedience as an important character, but, in fact, children get everything they want and nothing is expected of them at this stage.

Gender differences in Khalapur exist, but they are not overriding concerns. Childhood is basically a time of fun and freedom and as such, the demands on kids, whatever their gender, are slight.

Life for Gusii boys and girls in western Kenya is much less free. Each sex, according to Gusii custom, will be initiated by circumcision—boys at around ten years of age and girls a bit younger, at eight years of age.[19] Until they are circumcised, children are considered "inferior." The period from weaning to initiation is the time when children learn to be adults, a time when parents and others make sure they know how to act. Children who can walk and talk, the Gusii believe, must be repeatedly punished to learn correct, obedient behavior and there is nothing about them that deserves respect; children are of the lowest social status. The Gusii is a hierarchical society in which respect and obedience are the main parental objectives. Children, of course, know how to work this system. Anthropologist Robert LeVine, who has worked with the Gusii since the 1950s, puts it this way: "The lessons (to children) are: Look down, don't initiate speech, don't talk back, do what you're told, and get away as soon as possible. . . . Some children become particularly skilled at evading parental authority; all have experiences not covered, or authorized, by the model."[20]

And yet Gusii children are considered family and household assets. Both sexes work in the fields, tend cattle, and care for younger siblings. Boys grow into adults and protect their parents and the community and bring in cash from outside jobs. They eventually bring wives into the homestead, which means more workers. Girls too are appreciated for their work before marriage, but once married they leave and live in their husband's homestead and contribute to his family. As children, however, they are tireless domestics and vital to the household, in that they allow mothers to work at other tasks.

The oldest uncircumcised girl is placed in charge of the younger children, and the oldest uncircumcised boy is placed in charge of the cattle. These jobs are important because Gusii women are occupied most of the day in the fields, at markets, and around the homestead. Kids are required to stick close to home when their mother is gone. They are restricted, but usually unsupervised most of the day. When boys herd cattle, smaller kids tag along and form playgroups. Since they are wandering around, any adult can check on their behavior.

By Western standards, these kids have significant responsibilities, and the expectations of their parents are comparatively high. Nor are children praised for what they do—to praise a child would be to spoil them, Gusii parents feel. Children are expected to do their job as a functioning member of the household compound. They begin working at an early age; by age three or so, they are already running errands and might even help in the fields. And as they grow older, Gusii kids move up the social hierarchy and take on more responsibility. As adults, men are dominant over women, and clearly Gusii children of both sexes see this and absorb it. The adult order is reinforced by the division of labor—girls do household chores and care for infants, while boys tend cattle, although kids of either sex can take over any chore when needed.

Other Gusii customs underline the difference between boys and girls. Girls are taught to dress and act modestly. By the time they are four, they are taught to sit in a way that hides their genitalia, and by the time they are six, these girls must wear some sort of covering. Boys, on the other hand, need not wear clothes or cover their penises until initiation, which means ages ten to twelve; the uncircumcised penis is considered immature and asexual and therefore boys need not bother covering it up.

And so the Gusii childhood is one that is defined by work, a dominance hierarchy in which children rate rather low, and a division of labor by sex. But they also have lots of fun, running around and playing. Although children may be silent around adults, they spend most of their day with each other with no one looking on.

Every culture has rules of behavior for each sex, and those rules intersect with notions of who is in charge and what children "should" be doing. All children model themselves after the same-sex adults, and in some cases, they are instructed or expected to do so. Our ways in the West, where we often segregate our children by age and sex, are unusual. We look for playgroups with children of the same age. And then girls attend ballet class, while boys learn to play hockey. In some grammar schools, boys sit on one side of the room and girls on the other. At home, the daughters sleep in one room and the sons in another. Even the computer games are genderized. What exactly are we trying to accomplish with this policy, we might ask?

Should We Have No Gender?

There is no society that is silent about gender. All cultures recognize that females and males are different, and that they "should be different." This difference is played out during infancy and childhood as parents dress their kids according to traditions of what is male and what is female, and as they mold their girls and boys in separate ways. A division of the sexes is so prevalent, so much a part of every culture, that it is one of the universals of human ideology and behavior. Does that make genderization "natural" and therefore "good"?

The real issue here is not being male or female, or looking and acting male or female, but how those genders are treated by others. Genderization is a political issue and that's because in all cultures gender is intertwined with power. And women in every society are the less powerful gender. It doesn't take a committed feminist to see that female adults do not fare well in many cultures; women are often not educated, they usually have no independent economic means, and they are sometimes restricted in their movements. In that sense, being one gender rather than the other is not just biological, it is political. And it is often oppressive. And that is why genderization counts. It doesn't matter that much that little girls are expected to tend babies and boys tend to get the cattle. But it does matter when those same girls are circumcised against their will, or feel they have no say in who they marry. It doesn't matter that little girls are dressed in pink and boys in blue, but it does matter when those same girls are told as young women to act nice, lower their ambitions, and stand aside as the men get the good jobs.

The point is that these gender divisions that seem so innocent at age six can grow into monsters at age twenty. And that's why as parents, we need to hold up that pink dress and think a bit—what is the lesson here for my daughter? How does the culture view her? How will she view herself if she spends the first six years of her life being told that girls should act nice? Maybe that dress could be green, brown, or blue. Maybe she should be encouraged to give the baby doll to her brother and spend the afternoon throwing his truck down the stairs. And maybe we should examine our assumptions as parents. Yes, kids need to know what sex they are, and they will be compelled to fit into a gender role that is appropriate for the culture. But that role need not be all-inclusive, and it need not be restrictive. When we free up our thoughts on gender roles, we not only free up our children to have goals and ambitions that are more broadly based but we also free up ourselves.

CHAPTER EIGHT

The Dark Side of Childhood

Kristen is four years old. She lives with her mother in a wooden house built on stilts. Clean laundry hangs on trees that dot the hard-packed mud yard, chickens run around, and a soft Caribbean breeze wafts the smell of roasting coffee beans across the porch. Behind the house, volcanic cliffs fall to the sea—every morning Kristen wakes up to a billion-dollar view of the Atlantic. On the surface, her life here on the island of Dominica seems like a slice of paradise.

But all is not so idyllic. Kristen's mother, Julianne, was single, away at school in the city, when she became pregnant with Kristen. Julianne had to move home and endure some family disapproval as a single mother. Recently, an old friend of her mother's, a nice guy named Robbie, became part of the household, a stepfather of sorts. And Julianne is not working nor planning to work anytime soon.

Kids

Like most kids, Kristen has stress in her life. It comes at home, at school, and with friends. But unlike most kids, her stress level, and its effect on her health, is being closely watched. For the past thirteen years, anthropologist Mark Flinn of the University of Missouri has followed the children in Kristen's village, Bwa Mawego,[1] documenting not only what they do but how they are. Using growth charts, saliva samples checking cortisol and immunoglobulin levels, health records from the local clinic, twice-weekly checks on who is sick, and the daily ethnography of their lives, Flinn is trying to figure out the relationship between stress and health in children. Unlike lab studies that take a one-shot view of stress, he hopes to cast a wide net across family dynamics, and over generations, to understand how each child navigates the ups and downs of life.

Flinn has discovered that family trauma, more than anything, affects the health and welfare of children, and there is family trauma no matter the culture, the country, or the family. More remarkable, he evaluates the darker consequences of human behavior not simply as a social ill that needs correction. Instead, Flinn watches kids through a lens that mixes biology and culture, a perspective that focuses not just on how the kids behave but *why* they act as they do from an evolutionary perspective.

In the past, social scientists assumed that the dark side of human behavior was a product of culture, that society makes its own demons and only social corrections will cure these social ills. Flinn is part of a group of researchers called evolutionary biologists who are trained in evolutionary theory and are taking another approach. They have recently demonstrated that much of the pain that children suffer follows what evolutionary theory might predict. Although such a perspective does not make the pain any easier, or morally correct, it does help piece together why childhood can be such a terribly difficult time for so many.

The evolutionary, or biological, approach adds a new piece to the puzzle of understanding how kids react to bad times and how so many of them rally after bad times. Taking the long view also helps predict which kids might be most at risk, thus providing a broad and meaningful context from which to protect those kids.

Kids Under Stress

Everyday events can be stressful to children. For some, school is not just boring but something to be avoided. For others, attempting to be successful at sports, or belonging to an in-group, or wanting to look a certain way can be stressful. Many grow up familiar with violence, either in the home or because of social unrest in their culture—civil war and political strife. In fact, the idea that childhood is a happy time, a carefree time, is a modern Western invention that comes with affluence. But even kids with affluent lives can buckle under because of stress. Stress is often a matter of perception, rather than actual fact.

Mark Flinn arrived on the island of Dominica in 1988. His previous work, on Trinidad, had focused on fathers and their role in child care (see section on stepparents). This time he wanted to focus on the kids and discover what made their lives stressful, and how they dealt with that stress. Poverty, he assumed, must be a great stressor. When kids come from poor households, they not only have less stuff—toys, books, clothing, entertainment—they also have less nutritious food, less decent health care, fewer chances of good education, and their parents are always under pressure to make more money. And so Flinn chose a rural village at the dead end of a road where only about half the houses have electricity and none have running water. Seven hundred people of mixed African, Carib, and European descent live there in about 200 houses made of wood or concrete block. Household composition, as is typical in the Caribbean, is fluid. Fathers go off-island for a time to find work in agricultural fields in the United States or Canada, or mothers work away from the village at resorts. Kids might live with their biological parents, stepparents, grandparents, or in houses with various relatives. More significant, Flinn discovered that these households are always dynamic—from 1990 to 1994, for example, 31 percent of the households with children changed composition at least once, and over the same period at least a quarter of the kids lived in more than one household.[2] But the individual households were also connected to each other by extensive kin networks, so that even when kids changed houses, they were still with relatives who knew all about them.

Flinn planned to take his work one step past the usual anthropological fare. He would do the traditional ethnography (that is, watching and talking to people), but this time he wanted to study their biology as well. It's possible to ask people how they are and to make your own observations, but only the body biologically charts what is going on. So Flinn sought some sort of biological measure that could track what kids were feeling—specifically, how they were reacting to stress. And he wanted a measure that was as noninvasive as possible. He could have asked kids to march into a clinic each day and take blood samples or urine samples from them. But would these kids really do that day after day? And wouldn't the very procedure affect the way they were feeling and elevate their stress response? Based on work that had been conducted in rural Africa on women and reproduction,[3] Flinn settled on an efficient and noninvasive measure of stress—the hormonal composition of saliva. What could be easier than asking kids to spit a few times a day?

Saliva, it turns out, contains cortisol, a hormone that is produced in response to stress. When a person perceives an uncertainty in life, and he or she doesn't know what to do, the body reacts. Cortisol modulates energy output, the immune system, and signals the mind to wake up. In other words, cortisol is the hormone that makes the body go on alert. And this is all good when the perceived threat is short term. "Without cortisol," explains Flinn, "humans can't endure the ups-and-downs of everyday life."[4] But over time, those same mechanisms break the body down. With persistent stress, the immune system is compromised, a person can't think well, and physical growth and maturity are slowed.[5] Eventually, long-term stress is implicated in autoimmune diseases, resistance to infectious diseases, and many other health problems. And so physiological alert systems that have evolved to help the body to deal with incidental threats turn out to be bad when the threat goes on for too long.

The effect of persistently high cortisol levels on children can be especially damaging. Children are constantly growing and yet the physiology of the stress response puts many of those developing systems on hold.[6] As energy is redirected to fend off a perceived threat and the stress continues over days or weeks, then those systems are deeply affected. In children, unusually high cortisol levels from constant stress slow physical growth and delay sexual maturity. In addition, elevated cortisol can slow the growth of brain cells.[7] Stress also dampens the immune system, which makes children prone to upper-respiratory infections and diarrhea, diseases that are often fatal at that age.[8] Also, stress carried into adulthood is deadly. "One reason to worry about stress in childhood is that this is the time when we learn how to manage stress, patterns that we will carry forward into our adult lives. And we don't take the hit on some of the health consequences until we are older," explains Megan Gunnar, an expert on stress in children at the Institute of Child Development, University of Minnesota. "Increasingly, we are finding that many of those adult diseases, the things that knock us down when we are forty or fifty—heart disease, high blood pressure, and so on—are detectable in childhood, the patterns are set."

And middle-class American kids can be just as stressed as kids living in rougher economic or social conditions. "There are lots of things in our overly busy lifestyles that make demands and exceed resources, calling on our kids to dig deep down and pull out more than they thought they could," says Gunnar. Scheduled activities, lack of sleep, and complex family lifestyles often leave little downtime. And then there are grades to worry about, performance anxiety, peer pressure. "Kids do have stressful things to manage; stress is not something to start worrying about in adulthood," Gunnar explains.

Flinn knew that if he could measure cortisol in the kids in Bwa Mawego, he would have some idea of their levels of stress. The complication was that personality and temperament are involved in how one perceives threat in the first place—an experience that might seem frightening to one kid might be seen as normal to another. Also, a child can habituate (that is, get used to stress when it occurs daily and their bodies stop reacting as strongly). And when the stressful event takes place during prenatal life or early infancy, various stress response systems can be permanently altered and hard to interpret in older children and adults. To further complicate matters, cortisol response is not the only physiological change that takes place during stressful situations, not the only hormone involved in psychological or social situations. And finally cortisol levels are also affected by food intake and time of day. But if all these variables are controlled, cortisol makes for a good benchmark, and one that can be easily collected and measured in a field situation, especially with kids.[9]

And so Flinn's methodology became a surprising mix of biology and culture. Every day, he and assistants would visit households and ask the kids to rinse their mouths with water, chew on a stick of gum to produce saliva, and then spit into a cup. Soon even the more shy kids took this in stride. And while the kids were spitting into the cup, the researchers asked them and their caretakers a series of questions. They asked about what the kids were doing and how they felt about their activities. They asked about their health. And sometimes the researchers followed certain kids all day and gathered observational data. By living in the village, talking with kids and their caretakers and observing their lives, Flinn was able to track just about everything that might affect these kids, their families, and their lives.

Today he has over twenty-five thousand samples of 287 children ages three months to eighteen years, some of whom are now adults and have been followed for thirteen years; on average, each child has spit into a cup 96 times. Most samples were gathered twice a day over a period of months; others more intensely, even hourly, while following a particular child throughout the day. The idea is to build a database on cortisol that spans all the temporal variations that can effect hormone levels—hour to hour, day to day, and over years. "The old dogma was that if you got a sample once a day, collected between 8 and 10 A.M., that was enough," says Flinn. "I've found that controlling for time of day is not enough. You need to know what a normal day is for that child, including when they woke up. You also have to have repeated measures, which is expensive and makes things complicated."

According to Flinn, that's why more occasional lab work is suspect: "If you have a tough kid who has habituated to the mundane, giving a saliva sample in a lab would be a bore. You need to know what happened to this kid the day before . . . is he burned out? What are his reserves? What's the context?"

After thirteen years of spending many months each year absorbed into the life on Dominica, the message from Flinn's data is clear. It is a message that has little to do with socioeconomic level, nutrition, education, or any of the ills that we feel plague society. Rather, it highlights the more fundamental issue of family stability. Flinn has documented over and over that when families experience some sort of personal trauma—say the father and mother have a fight, or the father leaves, or the grandmother hits a kid— the children react physiologically. Their cortisol levels rise and a few days later, they get sick. Kids are stressed by family quarrels, conflict among household members, and when they are physically punished by their caretakers. And boys and girls seem to experience these changes differently. When the mother or father leaves for a few days, even when the trip is expected, the cortisol levels of both sexes rise moderately. But as they get older, a mother leaving is harder on girls than boys.[10]

Flinn also found that household composition has an effect on the stress levels of the children. Kids who live with both biological parents have lower cortisol levels than those living with a mix of genetic and stepparents, or those living with one biological parent who has no kin support. There is a sex difference in this reaction as well. Boys from households without fathers have low cortisol levels in infancy and they grow more slowly than boys with fathers at home. A consistently low level in children or adults is not normal. This cortisol profile suggests an unhealthy, dampened cortisol response, which does not allow someone to cope with every day simple stressors. Stable parental relationships, or supportive kin networks, in other words, are crucial for kids. As Flinn concludes, "Family interactions are a critical psychosocial stressor in children's lives."[11]

And for those kids under chronic stress from continued family trauma, the picture is even more negative. There are two abnormal patterns of cortisol that Flinn can track straight to behavior problems. In one abnormal pattern, certain children have a low basal cortisol level interspersed with spikes of unnaturally high levels of the stress hormone. In addition, kids with this pattern also show what Flinn calls "blunted" responses to physical activities which would normally elevate cortisol. Some of these kids have been stressed since they were conceived, and they probably missed certain sensitive periods for obtaining normal cortisol profiles. These kids have diminished immune responses, are sick more frequently, exhibit fatigue, and don't play well or sleep well. They also have behavioral problems and are less sociable and more aggressive than kids with normal profiles. In the second pattern, children might have chronically high levels of cortisol, which is also not normal. In this case, the kids are shy and anxious, but just as unhealthy as the ones with the low levels with spikes of cortisol.

Permanent damage has also been seen in other kids who have lived under duress. Studies of Romanian orphans kept in appalling conditions who were then adopted into families in the United States show that the adoptees soon catch up in terms of physical growth and maturation. But those who spent the longest time in the orphanage, without affection, attention, or normal social interactions, continue to have major behavioral problems.[12]

One of Flinn's most disturbing findings is that children do not habituate to family trauma (that is, no matter how often it happens, the kids still react just as strongly when Mom and Dad fight). One might think that the body would get used to all this. But the evidence shows that kids are just as sensitive the first time as they are the tenth time a traumatic event takes place.

Sometimes it's not always that easy to see a direct, causal relationship between cortisol and behavior or health. Personality and temperament are involved in how one perceives threat in the first place—as noted earlier, an experience that might seem frightening to one kid might be seen as normal to another. The key seems to be predictability, from the child's point of view. Researchers have found that cortisol levels of British children are lower at school, where life is predictable and stable, and higher at home, where they believe anything can happen.[13] And other studies of parents in Western culture who are unresponsive to kids, or where martial strife is daily fare, show that home life can be very stressful to kids and it can affect their health and behavior in the long term.[14]

As Flinn sees it, the family is supposed to be a physical and social resource for children. Human infants and children are highly dependent creatures, and their caretakers are designed to respond to their signals and help them navigate life until they are fully independent.[15] But sometimes caretakers are not good at this role. And children, as Flinn explains, are designed to be highly sensitive to family issues, so it's no wonder they are so traumatized by family upsets. It's also important to realize that the impact of stress on children in a small village in the Caribbean is only an example of how stress affects children everywhere. Family trauma and how it affects children, in other words, is a human universal.

Oddly enough, it might be argued that the social system advocated in the West—the nuclear family—makes kids even more vulnerable to the ups and downs of family life. In the Caribbean and most other less industrialized countries and regions, families are composed of extensive kin networks. As such, kids in those systems have many more relatives to call on. Single parents usually have their own parents in the household, or living close by. If the father leaves the family, there are grandfathers, uncles, and cousins to fill the gap. Kids can leave the house when Mom and Dad are fighting and walk down the street to hang out with Grandma. In Bwa Mwego, for example, children with many kin connections have both higher weight and height for their age than kids with few relatives.[16] In that sense, these poor kids may be richer than kids in industrialized affluent nations when it comes to dealing with stress, and this may be the area that really counts for a healthy and happy life.

What makes this information so important is that it gets at the core of what it means to be a child. In the West, we expect our kids to be independent and self-reliant, not rocked by machinations of others. But millions of years of evolution have designed an organism that needs to be entwined with a family system with stable caretakers. When that expectation is not met, kids suffer and their lives are forever affected. Flinn's work and that of others is showing that the effects are a complex mix of biology, psychology, and behavior, and the effects are deeply felt and permanent.

The Favorite Child

All parents want what is best for their children. Or do they? In America—in theory, an egalitarian society—children are nonetheless treated differently according to gender—male children inherit the majority of the wealth, for example[17]—and parents frequently express strong feelings about the desired gender of an expected baby. Evolutionary biologists have discovered that this preference for one sex over another is nothing new—it is found in other animal species and across many cultures—and the offspring of one sex or another suffer because of this bias. More important, such sex biases sometimes make a sort of unpleasant evolutionary sense.

The specific gender of children shouldn't matter, since those offspring, regardless of sex, can have children and pass on the genes. And nature seems to know this. In most animal species, male and female offspring arrive at the same rate (that is, a ratio of 50:50). But sometimes, and under some conditions, one sex outnumbers the other. Biologists have found that these biases of sex ratio are related to the "cost" of producing each sex and the prospects of the parents.[18] If the parents perceive that they can better raise one sex or another, they sometimes selectively miscarry the "wrong" sex, or invest less in that sex once the baby is born.[19] For example, the South American rodent the coypu will miscarry female litters when conditions are good but keep small male litters because good times mean a mother can more easily raise big males to maturity. Those big males, in turn, will have a better chance of conceiving with available females.[20] Opossums do the same thing—when adult females are fed more food, they will produce 40 percent more male pups because they know times are good.[21] Such biases in sex ratios that vary according to maternal conditions or the mother's perceived physical or social environment have been found in such wide ranging species as laboratory mice, wood rats, and red deer among others.[22] Data from nonhuman primates is a little less clear, of course, because primates reproduce at a much slower rate and they most often have singleton births. As a result, each baby, each packet of genes if you will, is precious, no matter the sex. But still, there are times when mothers favor one sex over another. High-ranking spider monkey mothers tend to produce males and care for them longer than they care for female offspring. These favored males then stay in the group and enjoy high reproductive success, while low-ranking mothers produce females who leave their homes and have more risky reproductive futures.[23] In general, primates have to weigh their social rank and what the prospects might be for their kids way down the line.

The same type of considerations must come into play when human primates favor children of one sex over another; humans don't seem to be able to vary the ratio at conception very well, but they do differentially abort fetuses, practice infanticide, nurture babies, and pass on their wealth according to sex.[24] Female infanticide is common in some areas of India and in China. Anthropologist Sarah Blaffer Hrdy has documented that people have favored one sex over another all over the world and throughout time, and they continue to do so today. In societies that are characterized by strict social hierarchies, men usually control the goods and materials and men with more goods have higher status. These men also seem to have more children.[25] In these societies, it makes sense for high-status parents to try and have more sons and to favor sons over daughters. Daughters, in this class, are simply a waste of resources. In turn, the lower echelon might favor daughters because their sons would have no chance at all in competing with well-to-do sons, while their daughters might marry up.[26] In that sense, such practices are part of the social system, and it depends upon who has the best prospects of marrying, having lots of children, and passing on genes.

In some societies females, rather than males, are the favored sex. Anthropologist Lee Cronk has found that among the Cheyenne Indians daughters were more important than sons and in urban America in the nineteenth century daughters were also favored because girls could get jobs more easily than boys. Today the Kanjar people of Pakistan favor girls because they can be gainfully employed as dancers, sellers of crafts, and occasionally serve as prostitutes, all which provides the families with at least half their income. Girls are so valued that men must pay a high price, called bridewealth, to marry. As a result, baby girls are greeted with celebration at birth because they represent great economic potential.[27] There are additional examples from contemporary America to the Hungarian Gypsies in which circumstances are such that girls are the favored child and males are neglected.

These examples are important to Cronk. For years he has studied the Mukogodo people of central Kenya, where daughters, rather than sons, are the favorite.[28] The Mukogodo have an unusual history. Early in this century, they were an impoverished hunter-gatherers and beekeeping society that lived in caves in the Mukogodo Hills. They were isolated from other groups linguistically, socially, and spatially and chose to marry only with their own kind. During colonization, and because of population growth, they began to come into contact with various nomadic herders, such as the Maasai and the Sumburu. Eventually, the Mukogodo and these herders began to intermarry, and so Mukogodo men began to follow the rules for obtaining wives in the other groups—they had to obtain livestock to trade for a wife. The Mukogodo began to take on the values of the herders: They adopted their language, culture, and even their way of life. But this also meant the Mukogodo entered into this more socially stratified society at the bottom of the hierarchy. Relative to the more established groups, they had small herds of sheep and goats, the standard by which all pastoralists judge wealth and status; they are still considered savages by those they are trying to emulate. The more established groups call them *il torrobo,* which means "poor scum."

For Mukogodo men, their low status is an acute problem—they have trouble obtaining a wife, while men from the other group often have several wives. But for Mukogodo women, finding a mate is easy. Since Maasai-speaking groups are polygynous and a man can have as many wives as he can afford, women can easily find a husband. And their families gain a major bridewealth of livestock when they do. And so Mukogodo women marry and have more children than Mukogodo men.

What does this have to do with children? Quite simply, girls in this scenario are worth more than boys because they can always marry and have children, while boys are more of a liability. Cronk found that the favoritism toward girls is played out in the ways parents treat their kids. Although there seems to be an equal sex ratio at birth, and there is no evidence of male-based infanticide, girls seem to fare better over childhood—by the age of four, there were only 67 boys to every 100 girls. Why is there such a high mortality among boys? Cronk found that parents spend great effort and expense taking their daughters to the medical clinic, and they do this significantly more often than they take their sons. They also enroll their daughters more often in mission programs that provide food and child-care instruction to adults. Mothers breast-feed their daughters longer. Cronk saw several cases of neglect of boys (but not girls)—everything from malnutrition to festering wounds. And in a study in which Cronk focused on child-care practices and measures of child health among 40 kids, he found a definite favoring of girls. Mothers and other caretakers were consistently more solicitous toward girls; mothers of girls nursed their children more, held them more, and were physically closer to them than mothers of boys. The girls were also given better medical care, and they showed better growth performance than the boys. No wonder they were more likely to survive the rigors of early childhood.

The point is not to focus on favoring girls or boys, but to recognize the fact that parents really do make conscious decisions about favoring one sex over another. These decisions, in extreme conditions, can result in neglect, ill health, and sometimes the death of the less-wanted sex. While we might find such behavior theoretically amoral, all over the world such biased feelings and actions can be compelling. That compulsion, the evolutionary biologists remind us, may be part of human nature. Parents who favor sons because those sons will have social power and better reproductive success are making an appropriate evolutionary decision, upping their chances of passing on genes to the next generation. Those of low status and power might favor daughters for the same reason. Of course, just because actions make evolutionary sense, that does not make it right. But understanding the underlying mechanism behind a negative behavior should open the way for counteracting that reprehensible behavior in a real and permanent way. The way to end discrimination of children of one sex or another is to make the ultimate value of all children, regardless of sex, equal. And one way to raise the value of children is to value adults of each sex equally as well.

The Worst-Case Scenario

I can't possibly write about children and the dark side of their young lives without writing about child abuse and child homicide. Of course, there are any number of books and articles about child abuse in Western culture. And of course, others have analyzed and written about why it happens and what might be done to keep kids out of harm's way. What could the evolutionary framework that informs this book possibly add to this mountain of sociological studies and practical prescriptions?

Oddly enough, research by evolutionary biologists and anthropologists have provided some fundamental insights into kids at risk that are providing a helpful context for social workers, who are trying so hard to protect and save these kids.

From an evolutionary point of view, at least on the surface, hurting children makes no sense at all. They share their parents' genes and parents want them to grow up to reproductive age and extend their genetic legacy by having kids themselves. The family, in evolutionary terms, should be a safe place in which children are born, grow up, before having families of their own. But life is not that simple. As we know from the work that has been done on stress and children, family at times can be the least safe place of all, especially when the household erupts into violence. Mark Flinn's work has also shown that kids are especially affected by family trauma.

Some kids are more likely to be designated targets of violence than others. Evolutionary biologists Martin Daly and Margo Wilson have collected data on family composition and abuse of children in Canada from police records, telephone interviews, and national statistics. They have shown over and over that when abuse and child homicide occur, stepchildren are much more likely to be victims than children living with both biological parents or one biological parent.[29] In one study, for example, preschoolers living with one biological parent and one stepparent were forty times more likely to be abused.[30] There are other risk factors as well. The age of the mother, the stress of poverty, the perceived health of the child or baby (children with congenital deformities are disproportionately abused), and especially the age of the child (abuse decreases with age) can all point to problems. But none of these factors are as powerful a predictor of risk as genetic relationship. As Daly and Wilson put it, "Stepparenthood *per se* remains the single most powerful risk for child abuse that has yet been identified."[31]

Others have found similar findings in non-Western cultures. For example, Mark Flinn found when working in a village in Trinidad that stepfathers admitted they cared less for stepchildren than their biological children, and they were more likely to be antagonist toward nonbiological children. Even more significant, the children in this Trinidadian village brought up by stepparents ended up producing fewer living children than those brought up by biological parents, indicating a negative link to reproductive success even without direct abuse.[32]

For Daly and Wilson and others who have tracked these data, the increased risk that children with stepparents face makes biological, albeit very distasteful, sense. Human parents are required to invest enormous amounts of time and energy to raise children to adulthood. It is an investment that stretches over many years. Biological parents are compelled to make that investment in order to successfully pass on their genetic legacy. But stepparents share no genes in common with stepchildren; their level of commitment and concern, at least from an evolutionary standpoint, simply isn't the same.

With so many blended and reconstituted families in the West today, evidence of the increased risk of nonbiological children is alarming. Obviously, most stepchildren are not abused, and most blended families navigate their relationships just fine. But what Daly and Wilson and others show is that when a mother or a father brings in a new partner, there could be some rocky days ahead, and that shouldn't be so surprising. Biological parents should be aware of the risk of introducing a nongenetic parent and take serious and caring steps to make sure the transition goes smoothly. Denial, in this case, can be risky for kids and even dangerous.

Child Abuse Across Cultures

Sometimes it seems as if child abuse is purely a Western phenomenon—tabloids splash sensational cases in the media, statistics demonstrate that abuse is widespread, any number of federal, state, and country program are designed to find and help kids in trouble, and parents know that a concerned call to authorities from a stranger can potentially result in legal accusations and a child being whisked away into protective custody. Our paranoia is high on this issue, and it should be. But does that mean the West is especially rampant with child abuse and kids in other cultures are treated better? The answer is both "yes" and "no."

Parents in every culture believe they are doing what is "best" for their children. But "best" is a relative term, especially when considering traditional practices. For example, in the West, the "normal" model for infant sleep suggests that babies should sleep alone, in a crib, and sleep soundly and undisturbed all night. When parents in other cultures hear about this, they are appalled.[33] Babies in their cultures are held throughout the day, nursed whenever they are hungry, and sleep with their parents, and they could not imagine leaving a baby alone in a crib in another room to sleep. In fact, parents in many non-Western societies feel, because of the relative physical and emotional distance between Western children and their parents, that Westerners do not love their children and are not connected to them.[34]

At the same time, we in the West would consider it inhumane to force a child to vomit, or stay awake, be deprived of food, as part of a rite of passage into adulthood. But in those cultures where such ceremonies are important, these practices are considered necessary rather than abusive. Is that sense, some of any culture's traditional practices can be called into question.[35] Nowhere is this clash of culture more tricky than in the practice of female "circumcision," still practiced widely today in sub-Saharan Africa. In these cultures, girls only become "clean" and eligible for marriage when the part or all the clitoris is removed, and in some instances the vagina is sewn up. Those who do not practice this ritual are, of course, horrified at the idea of putting a young girl through such an operation (done without anesthesia) that causes not only great pain, the possibility of infection and subsequent infertility, but also the loss of sexual function. Is this abuse, or a cultural practice that's only the business of those involved? There is no easy answer to that question. The effects last forever and the operation can be fatal, and yet hundreds of women go through it willingly each year. Who, exactly, is going to step in and stop it?

Interestingly, people of all cultures have a set of norms and recognize that to go beyond those norms is to venture into child abuse. And as might be expected, in cultures where children are valued for their economic or cultural contributions, or because they represent a special kind of emotional satisfaction to adults, they are rarely mistreated.[36] On the other hand, when children do not fulfill those expected roles, they can be mistreated. Anthropologist Nancy Scheper-Hughes, working with mothers in Brazil's shantytowns where infant mortality is high, found that mothers assess the possibility of survival for each of their children and make what appear to be cold-hearted decisions about investing any effort and money in that child. If an unhealthy child dies, as expected, mothers are not blamed, and this is taken as a normal course of events.[37] Mothers throughout history and across cultures have always made these sorts of decisions about their young children, ending investment when there is little hope and moving on to allocating time and resources to their other children.[38]

In all cultures, there are particular characteristics that identify kids at greatest risk. In the West, low birth weight, deformities, developmental delays, and of course genetic relationship to caretakers are clear risk factors. Other cultures, those in which children are considered economic assets rather than burdens, as they are in the West, value some children more than others. Factors such as deformities, twins, illegitimacy, high birth order, and being one sex or the other can put kids at risk as well. Benign neglect rather than out and out abuse is often the way such disfavor is expressed. Anthropologist Jill Korbin writes that a perception of humanness can save or harm a child. In some cultures, once a baby has cried, or started nursing, or passes a certain age, infanticide is no longer an option.[39] Interestingly, poverty is not in and of itself a risk—yes, poor children get sick more often and die more often, but they are not abused or neglected more often than children of higher socioeconomic statuses. In fact, in third world countries where kin networks are stronger, children may be poor in material goods but less at risk for abuse because the culture values children. More significantly, these kids are cared for by any number of relatives. Under this type of more complicated support system, various people not only watch out for kids but intervene much earlier than in systems, such as the Western nuclear family, which is so socially isolated.[40]

Accounts of what children in various cultures go through is a testimony to the human imagination. For example, at five years of age, after spending all their time with their mothers, Bena Bena boys of New Guinea are taken away and held at a daylong ceremony in which their ears are pieced with a sharp pig bone. Eventually, they will move into the men's house and be virtually secluded from females of any age.[41] Other groups in New Guinea force young boys to practice fellatio on older males as a step toward manhood. In turn, at a certain age they will receive such favors, although upon marriage men rarely have sex with each other ever again.[42] Children in New Guinea are never harmed, and rarely punished, even though adults in many New Guinea societies are considered very aggressive and violent. Anthropologist L. L. Lanhness suggests that the lack of punishment comes from a societal belief that no one would presume to order someone else around, and they would never expect anyone to obey such orders anyway. And so adults are highly tolerant of bad behavior in kids and most often simply ignore it when children misbehave.[43]

In other societies, there is a mix of initial kindness during infancy followed by harsh treatment during early childhood. Jivaro mothers in Peru are initially very nurturing, but around eight months they begin to withdraw and soon leave the baby for hours without any food at all. Mothers are short-tempered and spank older kids or throw peppers into the fire and force the child to breathe this smoke until he or she passes out.[44] The Pilaga of Argentina start abandoning and ignoring their children as soon as they can walk. In general, these societies are characterized by interpersonal hostility; women have no power, which in turn seems to make mothers hostile toward their children.[45] And lest we forget, in the West, we coerce little ones into sitting at desks for hours at a time and focus on paper, expecting them to keep quiet, concentrate, and stay awake—something many cultures would see as sheer torture for children.

Clearly, child abuse and neglect cannot be adequately covered in one chapter. My point is to add to our thinking about kids and the dark side of childhood from a cross-cultural and evolutionary view. I have no prescription on how to define abuse or how to stop it. I only hope to broaden our view of what kids go through and suggest that sometimes bad things are done to kids in the name of culture, or society, or because tradition says it's okay. We know that there is no end to the ways in which adults force their ideas on children. In most cases, adults sincerely believe that such coercion will mold a certain kind of person or that the child "deserved" this treatment. More surprising is the fact that children respond in all sorts of ways to this negative handling. Some die from neglect or abuse, some are scarred physically or psychologically for life, some are simply molded to be quiet or obedient, and some are resilient to anything.

Bouncing Back

One amazing feature of human nature, and other animals as well, is resilience, the ability to return to balance after a trauma, or end up okay after long-term stress. But the quality of resilience is variable. Some individuals bounce right back, while others never recover or limp along permanently scarred. Given what many kids have to go through, resilience in children is a special feature, and one that has received much attention in recent years.

What makes some kids better able to handle the ups and downs of life? Why is that that some kids under the most difficult of circumstances turn out to have decent lives, while others are sucked under? Is there some way we can instill resilience in the vulnerable and at-risk kids?

The answers to those questions are not yet at hand. And this should come as no surprise. Humans are complex beings, both physiologically and psychologically, and from the moment of birth and through an extensive childhood, our flexible behavior is pushed and pulled by everything we experience. It is impossible to point to one thing—one gene, one personality trait, one support system, one experience—that can explain why some kids are more resilient than others. But still, there is some kind of magic there, and so researchers can't help but try to get a handle on its quality and variation.

Work in resilience began with studies of Western children with mentally ill or alcoholic parents. How were these kids affected and how come some of them were able to overcome this parental handicap? With such problematic parenting, surely these kids were very much at risk of turning out badly. But surprisingly, a certain percentage grew up just fine.[46] This work has been extended to children in other disadvantaged households, those living in poverty, or in urban areas full of crime and drugs, or in households where children were neglected and abused. And the results are the same. A certain minor percentage seem unaffected by their risky surroundings.[47]

Researchers have found that infants are quite good at recovering from unpleasantness—they do it every time they cry and a caretaker fixes whatever is wrong. This skill is maintained in life in some kids and adults. Resilience involves a whole range of systems, some biological and some psychological. In other words, it involves general outlook on life as well as such things as hormonal response. Resilient kids often have histories of being happy infants who cheerfully interacted with adults. They usually retain that positive approach to life, which in turn makes them easy kids to deal with. They also have specific coping skills that help them manage the details of a rocky life. In other words, some kids are born happy, charming, and resilient.

But there is one external factor that also seems to be critical for developing a sense of resilience—having a responsive caretaker early in life. Even kids who grew up under the worst conditions were able to deal with life in a positive way if they had at least one caretaker who paid attention to their needs and feelings and responded to their pain.[48] These responsive caretakers, researchers believe, can mediate any kind of emotional upheaval and be a supportive presence whatever transpires. And in the long term, such mediation helps teach a child that he or she can elicit a positive response in others—an invaluable social skill acquired under duress—thus build a sense of self-worth.

Children all over the world have to deal with poverty, stress, discrimination, and neglect. Some of them are physically or emotionally crippled, or lost, by these forces beyond their control. But even under the worst conditions, some go on to live happily, and even thrive in the face of adversity. Human nature is such that there must be mechanism to cope with hardships and difficulties in life. What is surprising is the youngest members of our species often come already equipped to handle these difficulties.

CHAPTER NINE

Childhood's End

There are now over 6 billion humans on this planet. When that 6-billionth child was born on October 12, 1999, UNICEF, an organization that ought to know since their aim is to protect children everywhere, warned that the statistical probability of that child reaching adulthood was rather low, especially since the child was born in South Asia, where the infant morality rate is about 50 percent.[1] UNICEF was trying to make a point—we might be amazed and proud of the fact that our species has reached such a mass of humanity, but we should also be ashamed that so many of our children, the most vulnerable among us, are at risk.

One third of those 6 million people are currently under fifteen years of age, and many of them live in poverty, don't get enough to eat, and are easy victims of disease, abuse, and war.[2] Three million children a year die from diseases that are preventable with vaccines, for example. Five hundred thousand children a year in sub-

Saharan Africa are infected with HIV each year and all will die of AIDS. Others are left orphans as the virus spreads across Africa.[3] Since 1990, 1.5 million children have been killed in aggressive armed conflicts, and at least 10 million more have been traumatized as witnesses to those conflicts.[4] And the bad news is not confined to underdeveloped or politically unstable countries. One in five children in the United States, the most affluent country on Earth today, lives in poverty; more than half the people who receive food stamps in this country are children; 15 percent of our kids have no health coverage; 50 percent will live in single-parent households during some part of their childhood.[5]

The kids are not all right.

As a society, as a culture, and as a people, we should take note. Yes, we should contribute to those agencies that support health and safety issues for children. Interestingly, Bill Gates, the richest man in America, and Ted Turner, who is also rolling in money, have chosen to fund massive immunization projects for children across the globe. As businessmen, they apparently see the huge payoffs from a reasonable investment—a simple shot and infant mortality goes down. But there are other, more local ways to work for kids. And some of these ways call for revolution in the way we think about our children, other people's children, and the role of culture in the way we raise our kids.

Trade-Offs

Every culture thinks it has the answer to the right way to raise children. Every set of parents is convinced that their way will bring up the most responsible, most successful, most well-adjusted citizens. Certainly as parents, we *hope* we're doing what is best. And yet every culture has its own, somewhat different agenda, and each parent has his or her own style. How can we all be doing what is "right" if there are so many ways to raise children? Each set of parents operates within a set of trade-offs that guide their behavior, trade-offs which are accepted without much thought because they seem so obvious. By trade-offs, I mean that each behavior has both a benefit and a cost; for every path taken, there is an alternate path that could also have been taken. In this book, I've tried to point out a number of different ways to think about how young children mature and develop. Some of the practices of other cultures are so different from the way most Westerners raise kids that they seem bizarre. Surely they cannot be applicable to our way of life. Yet much of how we as parents raise our children is culturally molded, unconsciously so at times, and therefore in need of examination. After considering the pluses and minuses of various practices and their effect on children, we may decide to reject or reconsider what our culture says is "right."

The Nuclear Family Revisited

Children in America today are most often born into a nuclear family in which one or both parents work outside the home. A third of children born in the United States are born to unmarried women, but still, that household is "nuclear" (that is, governed by an adult and not a household compound with extended kin networks). Just about everybody who works leaves home, and often kids are cared for by unrelated adults. There is institutional day care, preschool at ages three or four, and then regular required school from ages five on up. Many young children are enrolled in any number of programs outside the normal school day, taking classes in ballet or soccer or art lessons. This is the structure of early childhood in American culture today, and to most of us, it probably seems just right. After all, don't we bring up the smartest, most financially successful kids in the world?

But taking a wider view, there are trade-offs in how we raise our kids that affect our children's emotional and physical well-being. What we see as "normal" and "right" bears costs that parents should weigh against the benefits. There can be, in fact, an entirely different picture of our children's lives.

The nuclear family, for example, is accepted in this culture as the "best" family environment for children. Yet, one might ask, according to whom? Our ancient ancestors clearly didn't live in nuclear families.[6] Anthropologists suggest we come from a long line of people who lived in small kin-based groups that included several adult males and females. These adults made their living by foraging small game and vegetable matter from the forests and savannas. The members of these groups were presumably blood relatives (in most nonhuman primate groups, either the adult males or the adult females are closely related). The need for several adults was driven by a subsistence pattern of living, traveling from place to place to find enough to eat, as well as by the need to care for very dependent young. Our children, even as far back at 1.5 million years ago when brain size began to look more humanlike, needed several adults to care for them (see Chapter Two).[7] Although it might be politically correct today to think that mothers and the corresponding fathers of our ancestors alone cared for their children, it is more likely that women and their sisters and mothers performed the child care as well as provided youngsters with the majority of their calories.

Why is the way our ancestors raised children important to how we think of children today? We have come a long way away from the Pleistocene era of a million years ago. Surely our child-raising skills have evolved since then. Yes, but the point is that when we assume that the nuclear family is the "natural" way for parents and children, that word "natural" carries weight and has meaning. And in this case, it is wrong. The natural human child-care situation, the one through which our species evolved our minds and hearts, is a more communal, kin-based extended family system.

Recent work on the hunters and gatherer Hadza people of Africa shows that family means something very different from the nuclear family, at least when it comes to raising children. Hadza women have the highest reproductive success (that is, they are able to bring up the most children) when their mothers are still present to gather food for the whole family. In fact, it is traditional for nursing Hadza women to depend on their mothers (rather than their husbands) to bring home a bigger share of the food they consume.[8] In other cultures such as the Gusii, women live in household compounds that might include another wife, or sisters of her husband, and the women all watch out for the collective children. And when grandparents remain with the family, they become child-care workers as well.

Children seem to do well in a home life with more people than the nuclear family typically provides. In Rajput, India, for example, children display little sibling rivalry—anthropologists find little jealousy, yelling, or fighting.[9] The reason, anthropologists speculate, is partly because babies are taken in stride and are not the center of attention. So when a new baby is born, there is nothing to be jealous about. And the children have so many adults in the household to be with, so many people to talk to and be around, that there really isn't any reason to cry for special attention.

Given the chance, many Americans opt for this more extended family system as well. For example, grandparents are often integral to child care in this culture these days. *The New York Times* recently reported that one out of every ten grandparents is rearing a child or providing regular daily care for a child. And four out of ten grandparents see their grandchildren every week.[10] Even with our extended families broken into various homes, then, we still often see our parents as a resource.

I see this appreciation for extended family even among my friends. One household includes a grandfather, and our friends recognize that the only reason they could have a second child is that Grandpa does many of the household chores and babysits. Other friends live near sisters and brothers who regularly care for their child when they work. Even single parents are usually strongly connected to their families and use them as a child-care resource when possible. And when family is not around, we often try to substitute friends for family. My friend Carol regularly takes my daughter for the afternoon and does auntie things with her—they have tea parties or go for walks. This feels normal to me, Carol, and my daughter; a friend taking the place of extended family, occupying the space of one of my sisters.

And so while we accept the nuclear family in our culture, and many believe this is the *only* "right" system, it can also be very difficult. Mothers at home alone with two kids are exhausted and pushed beyond their physical and emotional resources. No wonder—our species didn't evolve to parent in isolation. One mother recently told me that she and her husband have found that the best adult to child ratio is three to one. The two of them plus one other adult or older responsible child make life run optimally even with one small child.

Our culture touts the nuclear family because of its supposed benefits—privacy for spouses, independence from grandparents, and the ability to control the destiny of your own small fiefdom. There is a tremendous pride of accomplishment when raising children without help. And we love the privacy of it all, the fact that no one has the right to interfere, that it's our turn to be in charge. But the costs for those with children are high—parental physical and emotional exhaustion and for the kids, fewer people to play with, earn from, and rely on. One could argue that there is a less substantial emotional foundation for kids. In the typical American way, we trade social and familiar networks for independence and privacy. While we gain a large measure of freedom. We exchange it for isolation, both for parents and for kids.

The Material Girl and Boy

In contrast to most other cultures, childhood in Western culture is seen as a special time of life, a time for fun and play. This stage in the human life cycle in our culture has been overwhelmed by special clothing, furniture, books, toys, and everything else under the sun. In America, the message seems to be that you aren't a good parent if your child doesn't have his or her own room filled with a mountain of stuff. But where does all this commercialism get us? Or our children? No one has shown that the amount of material goods one receives early in life has any effect on how an individual turns out as an adult. And no one has shown that kids with the latest toys are any happier than kids with less. In fact, most children would rather play with the adult version of whatever toy imitation one can suggest—offer a plastic saucepan or a real one to a child and see which one the three-year-old would rather play with.

They might not need things but they do need something to do. One of the most striking facts in this book is that children over the world work hard, except in Western culture. Older children do the majority of child care, and in all cultures but here, they run errands and help with domestic chores. Until very recently, Western kids also worked. They worked on farms or helped at home, and only the recent affluence of some levels of our culture has made childhood a freer time. Perhaps our children suffer from a lack of responsibility and they could be more involved in the household. Can a three-year-old dry dishes? Sure. Can he or she take laundry to his or her room? Why not? And any child who can reach the table can set out the silverware. We might even consider letting our seven- or eight-year-olds help out with the baby.

Day Care

American kids also differ from other cultures in that they are institutionalized early. On a recent visit to our local library, where they have storytime for toddlers, my daughter and I walked up to the sign-in sheet where she promptly grabbed a name tag and a pen, scribbled what looked to her like her name, peeled off the back, and slapped the name tag on the front of her pink-stripped overalls. At two and a half, she knew just what to do in that particular social situation. More of that kind of institutionalization comes in the form of day care and preschool.

When I was young, there was no such thing as day care and the idea of preschool was just catching on. Today there is a feeling in many communities that if a child over the age of twelve months is not in some sort of outside care or regular program, the parents aren't properly doing their job. And we often think that child care means taking our kids to day care centers or preschools and that all American kids are in this system. In fact, less than a third of children attend such facilities.[11] Most kids are cared for at home by parents, extended family members, or home care facilities where a mother is watching several children, including her own. And yet some toddlers go to preschool all day, five days a week, when parents work full-time; others attend part of the week, depending on the work schedules of their parents. And even when a parent is at home, many kids are put into programs to give the parent "a break," or so that they can get "something done," or because the parents believe this is necessary for socialization. The institution of day care is so accepted these days that it has become a major feature of our culture, and those who choose to be with their kids all the time are considered "old-fashioned."

I find this shift to accepting day care as "normal" one of the more fascinating cultural changes of this generation of parents. With both parents at work and no close relatives to fill in, there are

few other options for some. But is this optimal? we must ask ourselves. We seem to be re-creating a network of people for child
care, much as our ancient ancestors did. The only difference, and
one that might be critical, is that the modern network is not a web
of kin but a system of strangers who are hired for a job rather than
compelled by the dictates of genes to care for our kids. No one
knows what effect care by nonrelatives will have on our children in
the long term. It may be that good day care, with happy caretakers
who love children, is a benefit. These professional caretakers, who
we know are clearly not paid enough, are functioning as community members; if they stay at their jobs for years, they become familiars, like relatives. They may not have the genetic investment
to care for these kids, but they tend to like children, which is a
great benefit. Many parents who put their kids in day care believe
that a group situation is necessary for proper socialization. In a
culture where the birthrate is so low, they may be right. With only
one or two children at home, family life is not as full and rich as it
has been throughout human history. And it takes a lot of effort,
and sometimes money, to cart the kids to the pool and to the park
so they can interact with other kids. For a fee, day care then provides a regular kid-based play group that all kids crave.

But there are also costs to the day care option. As everyone
knows, good quality day care—facilities that are staffed by trained
and stable caretakers—is expensive and hard to find. Moreover,
kids don't always get the attention and nurturance they need, especially at this age. And sometimes the shifting internal sands at a
day care center add stress to their lives; many simply miss their
parents and what is familiar at home. Research shows that kids

who have been in this type of institutional care are more independent and self-assured than kids cared for at home. But they also
don't get along with other kids as well, are pushy, and don't resolve
disputes well. In other words, the idea of better socialization can
backfire.[12] And so there is a cost. Day care solves problems for parents, and good day care can be beneficial. But what children really
want, once they can talk and walk and are compelled to interact
with others, is to hang out with several familiar people in stable
environments. A culture that feels day care for toddlers who can
barely walk is acceptable, even important, needs to take a harder
look at this shift. What really is best for our children? Is this culturally based accommodation really in line with how young humans are biologically designed?

School Daze

We also have institutionalized the learning environment. In America, kindergarten starts at age five, and preschool, which is distinguished from day care by its educational bent, is initiated at age
three or four. Schooling, then, is *the* major learning environment
for children in America and other developed countries. Why do we
have so much school?

Most parents in America assume that education is the key to a
good life. And we assume that everyone else thinks similarly. Parents and communities in developing nations cry out for schools for
their children; women have worked hard to gain equal access to
the same education as men. People in developed nations spend bil-

lions of dollars on education and often believe that the cost of college is relative to the quality of the education and the probability of employment after college. But there are costs—not just financial ones—to putting kids in school for most of their growing years.

Before the dominance of the written word, there was no need to go to school—what would kids study without books? Children learned specific skills, of course, by imitation and by formal apprenticeships. "School has only been around for a short part of human history," as my sister once pointed out in commenting on my young nephew's inability to sit still in school. "Why do we think that the only way to learn is to sit at a desk all day, looking at a book?" Grammar school was established during the industrial revolution in the nineteenth century to educate kids about working in factories, and even then it was used primarily as a place to put kids when their mothers started working.[13] Before that, only rich kids with governesses learned from books. But once schools were established, they caught on. Here was a way for kids to learn to read and write and presumably work their way up the economic ladder in society to a better job. School was an equalizer. Today we expect our governments to build, maintain, and staff our school and we pay substantial taxes for them to do so. Education, in the form of school, is now the right of every citizen and this, we feel, is a mark of a civilized society. In America, in fact, the notion of universal education has been extended past high school to college, and more than one politician has stated that every American should have the right to a free college education.

Education is so universally lauded that it is risky for me even to point out some of the social and personal costs for our children. Let me be clear—good-quality education is a wonderful thing, and a way to have a rich, engaging, fulfilling life. But there are indeed costs. Robert LeVine, who works with the Gusii of western Kenya, has observed the transition from an era when few Gusii children went to school to today, when almost every child attends. In 1962, LeVine writes, 62 percent of the children attended school; by 1979, 95 percent attended, and many went on to the secondary school and university.[14] Gusii parents believe that such education is beneficial, but at the same time sending kids to school is a major change of life and culture. Children among the Gusii are seen as economic assets: They herd cattle and tend smaller children and perform domestic chores. With the older children gone from the household all day, the burden of such work reverts once again to women. Taking on Western values toward education, then, impacts Gusii life. Children can no longer take care of other children and they are gone from the homestead and removed from the control of their parents to an institution that guides their socialization. As a result, LeVine comments, the Gusii model of parenting with high fertility and many obedient children who contribute to the household is outdated.[15] It will be interesting to see if the Gusii will follow suit and change their parental style to match that of developed nations, where education and individual economic gains are what matters—and children are seen as burdens rather than assets. Will the fertility rate decline?

Other costs, those that are more familiar to Western parents, are harder to measure. Once in school, our children spend most of their waking hours with others. We have to trust in the personality, training, and specific goals of our schools and teachers and hope they match our own. And we have to be comfortable with the fact that complete strangers are a major influence on our kids. Then there is the issue of the institution itself. All institutions have agendas—some religious, some political, some historical. We have to accept that our kids will be indoctrinated into views of American history, independence, and attitudes that we might not agree with. Or put up with the teaching of subjects that we parents find baffling. Too much science? Too little art? No evolution? What about world geography? Once we give our kids up to the institution, we have to work to make the place our own or, as in some countries, accept the political or religious rhetoric along with the reading and writing. School, in other words, is not always an agenda-free institution.

Moreover, we have to live with the socialization process that the institution provides. Our kids soon learn at day care and pre-school how to stand in line. How to wait at the door. How to obey authority. Not that these skills are bad, but they are culturally bound, and therefore merit some thought. In contrast, a San child learns how to read a trail, how to find water, and how to carry a baby. What skills are taught in school merely because it's made up of many kids and a few authority figures? A friend enrolled his oldest boy in first grade in New Jersey one year. This boy has spent his first two years living with his parents in the bush in Botswana while his father, a primatologist, observed baboons for a research project. The boy has also lived in Ecuador and is currently being home-schooled in a remote part of Kenya. But during the year he attended normal school in New Jersey, his father said to me, "They sent home a list of the goals of first grade. I was stunned to discover that all of the goals were about getting along in a classroom. Nothing about learning this or that, just around sitting quietly, obeying the rules." In other words, much of the time the thrust of first grade was about discipline, what we might call socialization as a group, not about the individual child discovering new worlds.

And so it behooves us to think about what school as an institution presents to our children. It doesn't just provide education—the benefit—but also cultural expectations of behavior—sometimes at a cost.

And worries about this costs are legitimate. Reportedly, over 2 million children are now taking medication for depression, bipolar disorder, and various forms of attention deficit disorder.[16] Also, when behavioral problems are brought to the physician's office, especially ADHD, a child is now more likely to walk out with a prescription for drugs than a recommendation for counseling.[17] And so a growing number of young children are being medicated for behavior that parents, teachers, and physicians feel is inappropriate—but inappropriate to whom and in what context? Is the child who can't sit still at age three really maladapted or suffering from attention deficit disorder? If he weren't confined to a classroom, would anyone notice? In our culture, we force children into relatively rigid learning environments where it is necessary that they toe the line, that they become part of a group. And when we place children who are very young, say, between the ages of one to five, in this kind of environment, it is a lot to ask of an organism that is designed to run around at the peak of its metabolic rate. Perhaps we should think more about the animal drives we have at such ages, rather than the adult we hope to have someday. As anthropologist James McKenna says, "We in Western culture treat our children how we'd like them to become, not how they are."

Busy Kids

Another recent phenomenon that has also become the norm for today's children are planned activities. Everyone seems so terribly busy, so busy in fact that there is apparently a growing backlash against too many extracurricular activities. A recent *Newsweek* article described a group of parents in Minnesota who have formed a group, Family Life 1st, to support kids who cut back and spend more time with their families.[18] And so being too busy, too scheduled, deserves a closer look. Today we take our kids to play groups and sports lessons, Kindermusik and gym class, art instruction and Saturday puppet shows. All this running around, we parents think, will occupy, entertain, and yes, educate our kids. And surely it will. But such bustle also sets up a lifestyle that can become stressful for everybody involved. And stress, as we saw in Chapter Eight, can be harmful in and of itself. Packing too much into young lives may have benefits—we expose them to the myriad wonders of the world—but there are also costs.

And so it is useful to step back and look at what we expect of our children, and what we expect of ourselves as their guides through life. Is it really so important to be able to say your ABCs at age two? Is the best child the one who sits quietly rather than running noisily through the house? What exactly makes for a happy child?

Perhaps it is worth taking the time to question not only what we do with them now but also what we'd like them to become—successful in the traditional Western goals of independence and economic wealth—or just a happy and healthy individual.

Parenting Lessons

The other week I was looking for a new pair of glasses. So I went downtown to an optical shop. As usual, I had my daughter along. There were eyeglass frames and sunglasses all over the store, and being just over two years old, she was having a ball trying them on. The clerk came out of the back room and took one look at this scene and a sour look grew on his face. "She can't touch those," he said pointedly. And I responded that she was okay and wouldn't break anything. But he persisted, asking me to monitor her behavior and take the glasses out of her hands. "Those are very expensive," he said, and I again assured him that she would be very gentle. He turned away, exasperated with my bad parenting. He told me that he had just cleaned the frames that morning and she was not allowed to touch them. So I left. It's the kind of incident that any parent can encounter in Western culture, especially American culture. In many ways, we live in an antichild culture.

I recognize it because when we travel to other countries, more child-friendly places, the difference is amazing. In countries where the birthrate is higher, there are simply more children around. They play in the road, they accompany their parents everywhere, and no one seems to make a fuss that children are about. They are part of life, part of what adults do—have and raise children. But in

Western culture, children are the oddities. "Sometimes we feel self-conscious when we want to talk about how much fun we are having with our kids," says friend and fellow anthropologist Adam Clark Aracdi, a father of two boys who takes responsibility for much of their care. "Everyone seems to just complain about their kids in this culture; that's the accepted way to talk about them, but we are having a blast." We also seem to have forgotten that we were all once children. Instead, we act as if kids were aliens from another planet, or another time, and that the younger members of our species have nothing to do with us.

And so I end with this thought. In America today, we live in the culture with a low birthrate. There just aren't that many kids around and if you don't have children yourself, you can go days, even weeks, without interacting with a child. Also, we sequester children into special activities—entertainment and classes—that are away from most of adult society. We also separate ourselves by the very role of parent. "The world is divided into those who have children and those who don't," a friend once told me. People with kids tend to socialize together, knowing that their friends without kids probably don't have the patience for the chaos that comes with an evening around children. Instead, they save those friends for a night when the babysitter is available. Add to that the fact that children are not always acceptable in public places, such as restaurants, theaters, and shops. Kids are, in fact, invisible in much of our culture. We are not "used" to children, so they are not "used" to being part of our society day-to-day. In the end, we all lose out. Not everyone should have kids, but wouldn't it be wonderful if everyone could, at some level, enjoy the experience of children? Other cultures teach us that children can be an interesting, integral, part of society. We could, as a community and as a culture, enjoy this life stage more by simply having children around. Childhood has a special place in the human life course, and we should celebrate this time. We should, after all, have great empathy for children. We used to be kids ourselves, didn't we?

Notes

CHAPTER ONE: Kids' World

1. The San are sometimes referred to as "bushmen" by non-San, but this is considered a derogatory term.
2. Lee 1976.
3. Barr 1995.
4. Draper 1976; Draper and Cashdan 1988.
5. / indicates clicks. Imagine striking your tongue on the roof, or back or sides of your mouth as you pronounce words. These clicks are integral to the language of the San.
6. Draper 1976.
7. Blurton-Jones, Smith, et al. 1992; Blurton-Jones 1993; Woodburn 1968.
8. Woodburn 1968.
9. Hawkes, et al. 1989.
10. Blurton-Jones 1993.
11. See *Our Babies, Ourselves* for a discussion of how parenting styles are molded.
12. Hawkes, O'Connell, et al. 1995.
13. Blurton-Jones, Hawkes, et al. 1989; Blurton-Jones 1993.
14. Kramer 1998; Kramer (in press).
15. Kramer 1998, p. 318.
16. Barry and Paxson 1971.

17. Weisner and Gallimore 1977.

18. Weisner and Gallimore 1977.

19. Weisner and Gallimore 1977.

20. From the younger child's perspective, this is a situation in which they learn and are socialized. In a recent book, Jean Harris claims the peers are the major influence on the development of children. Although Harris's claim has some cross-cultural validity, applying this statement to the West misses the point. Multi-age child groups are a major influence on little kids where sibling care is the norm. But in the West, parents are the primary caretakers and therefore the primary influence.

21. Munroe, Munroe, et al. 1984.

22. White 1975.

23. James, Jenks, et al. 1998.

24. White 1975.

25. Ariès 1962; Humphries, Mack, et al. 1988; Postman 1982.

26. Lovejoy 1981.

27. Zeller 1994.

28. Postman 1982.

CHAPTER TWO: The Evolution of Childhood

1. Pereira and Fairbanks 1993.

2. Bogin 1997.

3. Bogin 1997; Bogin 1998; Panter-Brick 1998.

4. James 1998.

5. Isbell and Young 1995.

6. Rodman and McHenry 1980.

7. Small 1998.

8. Cheney, Seyfarth, et al. 1986.

9. Wrangham, McGrew, et al. 1994.

10. Bogin 1998.

11. Bogin 1997.

12. Bogin 1997.

13. Lee, Mayluf, et al. 1991.

14. Small 1998.

15. Note that at least half the babies in industrialized nations are bottle-fed and thus cannot enter into this description, since they already can be fed by someone other than the mother.

16. Dettwyler 1995 and Lee, Mayluf, et al. 1991.

17. Lancaster and Lancaster 1983.

18. Zeller 1994.
19. Zeller 1994.
20. Hawkes 1998; Hawkes 1999.
21. See also Blaffer Hrdy 1999.
22. Harvey, Martin, et al. 1987; Martin 1983.
23. Small 1998.
24. For an explanation of the head size/bipedal pelvis in human evolution and its consequences, see Small 1998.
25. Rosenberg 1992; Rosenberg and Trevethan 1995/96.
26. Bogin 1997; Bogin 1998.

CHAPTER THREE: Growing Up

1. Sinclair 1985.
2. Tanner 1990.
3. Sinclair 1985.
4. Bass 1971.
5. Bass 1971.
6. Tanner 1990.
7. Sinclair 1985.
8. Tanner 1990.
9. Tanner 1990.
10. Bogin 1999.
11. Smith 1992.
12. Barnet and Barnet 1998.
13. Sinclair 1985.
14. Barnet and Barnet 1998.
15. Bogin 1999; Tanner 1990.
16. Bogin 1999.
17. Bogin 1995; Shapiro 1939; Lasker 1952.
18. Billewicz and McGregor 1982; Harrison, Tanner, et al. 1988.
19. Panter-Brick 1997.
20. Habicht, Yarbrough, et al. 1974; Bogin 1999.
21. North American infants are fatter than other babies. They are born heavier and immediately fatter, but this may be due to the high proportion which are fed artificial milk rather than breast milk. In terms of health, such fatness may not be optimal.
22. Bogin 1999.
23. Takahashi 1984.
24. Jenkins, Orr-Ewing, et al. 1984.

25. See, for example, Bailey, Gershoff, et al. 1984; Billewicz and McGregor 1982.
26. Billewicz and McGregor 1982; Tanner 1990.
27. Shelov 1998.
28. Miller and Valman 1997.
29. Leach 1989; Brazelton 1992.

CHAPTER FOUR: Kidspeak

1. Hauser 1997.
2. Mitani 1985.
3. Cheney and Seyfarth 1990.
4. Gouzoules, Gouzoules, et al. 1984.
5. For a history of these projects, see Savage-Rumbaugh 1986.
6. Dunbar 1996.
7. Deacon 1997.
8. Cartmill 1998; Lieberman 1991.
9. Barnet and Barnet 1998.
10. Hauser 1997.
11. Barnet and Barnet 1998.
12. Barnet and Barnet 1998.
13. Deacon 1997.
14. See Barnet and Barnet 1998 for a wonderful explanation of language and neurophysiology, including the new techniques for research.
15. Barnet and Barnet 1998.
16. Dunbar 1996.
17. Calvin and Bickerson 2000.
18. Burling 1986; Wynn 1988.
19. Dunbar 1996.
20. Burling 1986.
21. Deacon 1997.
22. Bickerson 1990; Foley 1991.
23. Gannon and Holloway 1998.
24. Cronk 1999.
25. Chomsky 1977.
26. Ochs and Schieffelin 1984.
27. Barnet and Barnet 1998.
28. Barnet and Barnet 1998; Pinker 1994.
29. Pinker 1994.
30. For a clear explanation of language acquisition, see Golinkoff and Hirsh-Pasek 1999.

31. Bowerman 1985.

32. Lieberman 1991.

33. Pinker 1994.

34. Aitchison 1981.

35. Barnet and Barnet 1998.

36. Curtiss 1977.

37. Bickerson 1990.

38. Barnet and Barnet 1998.

39. Hart and Risley 1995.

40. Barnet and Barnet 1998.

41. LeVine, Dixon, et al. 1994. See also *Our Babies, Ourselves.*

42. Barnet and Barnet 1998.

43. Pinker 1994.

44. Pinker 1994.

45. Barnet and Barnet 1998.

46. Shelov 1998.

47. Barnet and Barnet 1998.

48. Shelov 1998.

49. Foley 1991.

50. Ochs and Schieffelin 1984.

51. Foley 1991.

52. Ochs and Schieffelin 1984.

53. Schieffelin 1990.

54. Ochs and Schieffelin 1984, p. 288.

55. Schieffelin 1990, p. 239.

56. Harkness 1990.

57. Schieffelin 1986.

58. LeVine, Dixon, et al. 1994.

59. Schieffelin 1990.

60. Foley 1991.

61. Gleason 1987.

62. Anderson 1986.

63. Ervin-Tripp, O'Connor, et al. 1984.

64. Ervin-Tripp and Mitchell-Kernan 1977.

65. Foley 1991.

66. Bernstein 1971.

CHAPTER FIVE: What Kids Know

1. Any text on child development would explain these principles. I used Mussen, Conger, et al. 1990.

2. Mussen, Conger, et al. 1990.

3. Kuczynski, Zahn-Waxler, et al. 1987.

4. Byrne 1995.

5. Byrne 1995.

6. Byrne 1995.

7. Byrne and Whiten 1988.

8. Byrne 1995.

9. Lewis and Brooks-Gunn 1979.

10. de Waal 1996.

11. de Waal 1996.

12. de Waal 1996, p. 61.

13. Gopnik, Meltzoff, et al. 1999.

14. See Gopnik, Meltzoff, et al. 1999 for a nice history of how these different theories have each had their day.

15. Gopnik, Meltzoff, et al. 1999, p. 59.

16. Harkness and Super 1997.

17. Postman 1982.

18. Levy 1996.

19. Levy 1996, p. 128.

20. LeVine, Dixon, et al. 1994.

21. LeVine, Dixon, et al. 1994, p. 90.

22. Rosenthal 1992.

23. Ben-Ari 1997.

24. Lewis 1995.

25. Lewis 1995.

26. Tobin, Wu, et al. 1989.

27. Tobin, Wu, et al. 1989.

CHAPTER SIX: Little Citizens

1. Cole and Cole 1996.

2. Small 1998.

3. Smuts 1985.

4. Belsky, Strinberg, et al. 1991.

5. de Waal 1996.

6. Kohlberg 1981.

7. Damon 1999.

8. Nucci and Turiel 1978.

9. de Waal 1990.

10. For an excellent discussion on the evolution of morality, see de Waal 1996.

11. Damon 1990; Damon 1999.

12. Small 1998.

13. LeVine 1974; LeVine, Dixon, et al. 1994.

14. Turnbull 1983.

15. Turnbull 1983, p. 45.

16. Morton 1996.

17. Morton 1996, p. 72.

18. Morton 1996, p. 73.

19. Peisner 1989.

20. Peisner 1989.

21. Peisner 1989, p. 138.

22. Peisner 1989.

23. Mussen, Conger, et al. 1990.

24. Cole and Cole 1996.

25. Mussen, Conger, et al. 1990.

CHAPTER SEVEN: Girls and Boys

1. For a description of the why of sex, see Small 1995 or Jolly 2000.

2. Maccoby 1998.

3. For a nice description of AIS, see Angier 1999.

4. Maccoby 1998.

5. Cole and Cole 1996.

6. Mussen, Conger, et al. 1990.

7. Mussen, Conger, et al. 1990.

8. Maccoby 1988; Maccoby 1998.

9. Maccoby 1998, p. 101.

10. Maccoby 1988; Maccoby 1998.

11. Whiting and Edwards 1988.

12. Maccoby 1998.

13. Miller 2000.

14. Whiting 1963; Whiting and Whiting 1975.

15. Whiting and Edwards 1988, p. 86.

16. Edwards 1993.

17. Whiting and Edwards 1988, p. 226.

18. Minturn and Hitchcock 1963.

19. LeVine and LeVine 1963.
20. LeVine, Dixon, et al. 1994.

CHAPTER EIGHT: The Dark Side of Childhood

1. The name of the village in Dominica and names of villagers have been changed.
2. Flinn and England 1995.
3. Ellison 1988.
4. Flinn and England 1995, p. 854.
5. Flinn and England 1995.
6. Sapolsky, per. com.
7. Sapolsky 1994.
8. Flinn 1995.
9. Flinn, Quinland et al. 1996.
10. Flinn, Quinland, et al. 1996.
11. Flinn and England 1995.
12. See Rutter info.
13. Long 1993.
14. Gottman 1989.
15. See Small 1998 for a full discussion of this co-evolved relationship.
16. Flinn et al., 1996.
17. Blaffer Hrdy 1999.
18. Fisher 1930. And see Cronk 1991b for a detailed explanation of this theory.
19. Trivers and Willard 1973.
20. Gosling 1986.
21. Austad and Sunquist 1986.
22. Blaffer Hrdy 1987; Blaffer Hrdy 1999.
23. McFarland Symington 1987.
24. Blaffer Hrdy 1999.
25. Blaffer Hrdy 1999.
26. Dikeman 1979.
27. Berland 1987. And see Cronk 1993 for an overview of these examples.
28. Cronk 1989; Cronk 1991a; Cronk 1991b; Cronk 1993.
29. Daly, Wilson, et al. 1980; Daly and Wilson 1985; Daly and Wilson 1988; Wilson and Daly 1987.
30. Daly and Wilson 1985.
31. Daly and Wilson 1988, p. 88.
32. Flinn 1988.
33. LeVine, Dixon, et al. 1994; Small 1998.

34. Korbin 1981; Lanhness 1981.
35. Korbin 1981; Korbin 1987.
36. Korbin 1987.
37. Scheper-Hughes 1992.
38. Blaffer Hrdy 1999.
39. Korbin 1981. The current argument in the United States over abortion rights follows this line of humanness.
40. Korbin 1981.
41. Lanhness 1981.
42. Lanhness 1981 and Kirkpatrick n.d.
43. Lanhness 1981.
44. Johnson 1981.
45. Johnson 1981.
46. Anthony and Cohler 1987; Dugan and Coles 1989; Werner and Smits 1989.
47. See, for example, the entire Volume 5 of *Developmental Psychopathology,* 1993.
48. Egeland, Carlson, et al. 1993.

CHAPTER NINE: Childhood's End

1. UNICEF news and information.
2. Small 1998.
3. UNICEF news and information.
4. Save the Children news and information.
5. Children's Defense Fund and the U.S. Census Bureau.
6. Jolly 2000.
7. Walker and Shipman 1997.
8. Hawkes 1998.
9. Minturn and Hitchcock 1963.
10. Lewis 2000.
11. Report from the Ann E. Casey Foundation on family child care, 2000.
12. Cole and Cole 1996.
13. Postman 1982.
14. LeVine, Dixon, et al. 1994.
15. LeVine, Dixon, et al. 1994.
16. Sachs 2000.
17. Gibbs 1998.
18. Kantrowitz 2000.

Bibliography

Aitchison, J. (1981). *Language Change: Progress or Decay?* New York, Universe Books.

Anderson, E. (1986). The acquisition of register variation by Anglo-American children. *Language Socialization Across Cultures.* B. B. Schiefflin and E. Ochs. Cambridge, Cambridge University Press: 153–61.

Angier, N. (1999). *Woman: An Intimate Geography.* New York, Houghton Mifflin.

Anthony, E. J., and B. J. Cohler (1987). *The Invulnerable Child.* New York, The Guilford Press.

Ariès, P. (1962). *Centuries of Childhood.* New York, Alfred A. Knopf.

Austad, S., and M. E. Sunquist (1986). "Sex-ratio manipulation in the common opossum." *Nature* 324: 58–60.

Bailey, S. M., S. N. Gershoff, et al. (1984). "A longitudinal study of growth and maturation in rural Thailand." *Human Biology* 56: 539–57.

Barnet, A. B., and R. J. Barnet (1998). *The Youngest Minds.* New York, Simon & Schuster.

Bibliography

Barr, R. G. (1995). "The enigma of infant crying: The emergence of defining dimensions." *Early Development and Parenting* 4: 225–32.

Barry, H., and L. M. Paxson (1971). "Infancy and early childhood: Cross-cultural codes 2." *Ethnology* 10: 466–508.

Bass, W. M. (1971). *Human Osteology: A Laboratory and Field Manual of the Human Skeleton.* Columbia, Missouri Archaeological Society.

Belsky, J., L. Strinberg, et al. (1991). "Childhood experience, interpersonal development, and reproductive strategy; An evolutionary theory of socialization." *Child Development* 62: 647–70.

Ben-Ari, E. (1997). *Japanese Childcare: An Interpretive Study of Culture and Organization.* London, Kegan Paul International.

Berland, J. C. (1987). Kanjar social organization. *The Other Nomads: Peripatetic Minorities in Cross-Cultural Perspective.* A. Rao. Köln, Böhlau Verlag: 247–65.

Bernstein, B. (1971). *Classes, Codes and Control.* London, Routledge and Kegan Paul.

Bickerson, D. (1990). *Language and Species.* Chicago, University of Chicago Press.

Billewicz, W. Z., and I. A. McGregor (1982). "A birth-to-maturity longitudinal study of heights and weights in two West African (Gambian) villages, 1951–1975." *Annals of Human Biology* 9: 309–20.

Blaffer Hrdy, S. (1987). Sex-biased parental investment among primates and other mammals: A critical evalution of the Triver-Willard Hypothesis. *Child Abuse and Neglect: Biosocial Dimensions.* R. J. Gelles and J. B. Lancaster. New York, Aldine de Gruyter: 97–147.

——— (1999). *Mother Nature: A History of Mothers, Infants, and Natural Selection.* New York, Pantheon.

Blurton-Jones, N. G. (1993). The lives of hunter-gatherer children: Effects of parental behavior and parental reproductive strategy. *Juvenile Primates.* M. E. Pereira and L. A. Fairbanks. Oxford, Oxford University Press: 309–26.

———, K. Hawkes, et al. (1989). Modelling and measuring costs of children in two foraging societies. *Comparative Socioecology.* V. Standen and R. Foley. Oxford, Blackwell: 367–90.

Bibliography

————, L. C. Smith, et al. (1992). "Demography of the Hadza; An increasing and high-density population of savanna foragers." *American Journal of Physical Anthropology* **89**: 159–81.

Bogin, B. (1995) Plasticity in the growth of Mayan refugee children living in the United States. *Human Variability and Plasticity.* C.G.N. Mascie-Taylor and B. Bogin. Cambridge, Cambridge University Press: 46–74.

———— (1997). "Evolutionary hypotheses for human childhood." *Yearbook of Physical Anthropology* **40**: 63–89.

———— (1998). Evolutionary and biological aspects of childhood. *Biosocial Perspectives on Children.* C. Panter-Brick. Cambridge, Cambridge University Press: 10–44.

———— (1999). *Patterns of Human Growth.* Cambridge, Cambridge University Press.

Bowerman, M. (1985). What shapes children's grammars? *The Crosslinguistic Study of Language Acquisition. Vol. 2.* D. I. Slobin. Hillsdale, Lawrence Erlbaum Associates: 1257–319.

Brazelton, T. B. (1992). *Touchpoints.* New York, Addison-Wesley.

Burling, R. (1986). "The selective advantage of complex language." *Ethology and Sociobiology* **7**: 1–16.

Byrne, R. (1995). *The Thinking Ape.* Oxford, Oxford University Press.

———— and A. Whiten (1988). *Machiavellian Intelligence: Social Expertise and the Evolution of Intelligence in Monkeys, Apes, and Humans.* Oxford, Clarendon Press.

Calvin, W. H., and D. Bickerton (2000). *Lengria ex Machina: Reconciling Darwin and Chomsky with the Human Brain.* Cambridge, M.I.T. Press.

Cartmill, M. (1998). "The gift of gab." *Discover* November: 56–64.

Cheney, D. L., and R. M. Seyfarth (1990). *How Monkeys See the World.* Chicago, University of Chicago Press.

———— et al. (1986). "Social intelligence and the evolution of the primate brain." *Science* **243**: 1361–66.

Chomsky, N. (1977). *Reflections on Language.* Glasgow, Fontana/Collins.

Cole, M., and S. R. Cole (1996). *The Development of Children.* New York, W. H. Freeman and Co.

Cronk, L. (1989). "Low socioeconomic status and female-biased parental invest-ment: The Mukogodo example." *American Anthropologist* 91: 414–29.

———— (1991a). "Intention versus behavior in parental sex preferences among the Mukogodo of Kenya." *Journal of Biosocial Science* 23: 229–40.

———— (1991b). "Preferential parental investment in daughters over sons." *Human Nature* 2: 387–417.

———— (1993). "Parental favoritism toward daughters." *American Scientist* 81: 272–79.

———— (1999). *That Complex Whole.* Boulder, Westview.

Curtiss, S. (1977). *Genie: A Psycholinguistic Study of a Modern-Day "Wild Child."* New York, Academic Press.

Daly, M., and M. Wilson (1985). "Child abuse and other risks of not living with both parents." *Ethology and Sociobiology* 6: 197–210.

———— (1988). *Homicide.* New York, Aldine de Gruyter.

———— et al. (1980). "Household composition and risk of child abuse and ne-glect." *Journal of Biosocial Science* 12: 333–40.

Damon, W. (1990). *The Moral Child: Nurturing Children's Natural Moral Growth.* New York, Free Press.

———— (1999). "The Moral Development of Children." *Scientific American* 281: 72–75.

Deacon, T. (1997). *The Symbolic Species: The Co-Evolution of Language and the Brain.* New York, W. W. Norton.

Dettwyler, K. A. (1995). A time to wean: The hominid blueprint for the natural age of weaning in modern human populations. *Breast-feeding: Biocultural Per-spectives.* P. Stuart-Macadam and K. A. Dettwyler. New York, Aldine de Gruyter: 39–73.

de Waal, Frans (1990). *Peacemaking Among Primates.* Cambridge, Harvard Univer-sity Press.

———— (1996). *Good Natured: The Origins of Right and Wrong in Humans and Other Animals.* Cambridge, Harvard University Press.

Dikeman, M. (1979). "The ecology of mating systems in hypergynous-dowery so-cieties." *Social Science Information* 18: 163–95.

Bibliography

Draper, P. (1976). Social and economic constraints on child life among the !Kung. *Kalahari Hunter-Gatherers.* R. B. Lee and I. DeVore. Cambridge, Harvard University Press.

―――― and E. Cashdan (1988). "Technological change and child behavior among the !Kung." *Ethnology* 27: 339–65.

Dugan, T. F., and R. Coles (1989). *The Child in Our Times: Studies in the Development of Resilience.* New York, Brunner/Mazel.

Dunbar, R. (1996). *Grooming, Gossip, and the Evolution of Language.* Cambridge, Harvard University Press.

Edwards, C. P. (1993). Behavioral sex differences in children of diverse cultures: The case of nurturance to infants. *Juvenile Primates.* M. E. Pereira and L. A. Fairbanks. Oxford, Oxford University Press: 327–38.

Egeland, B., E. Carlson, et al. (1993). "Resilience as process." *Developmental Psychopathology* 5: 517–28.

Ellison, P. (1988). "Human salivary steroids; Methodological considerations and applications in physical anthropology." *Yearbook of Physical Anthropology* 31: 115–42.

Ervin-Tripp, S., and C. Mitchell-Kernan (1977). *Child Discourse.* New York, Academic Press.

Ervin-Tripp, S., M. O'Connor, et al. (1984). Language and power in the family. *Language and Power.* C. Kramarae, M. Schulz and W. O'Barr. Newbury Park, Sage Publications: 116–35.

Fisher, R. A. (1930). *The Genetical Theory of Evolution.* New York, Dover.

Flinn, M. V. (1988). "Step- and genetic parent/offspring relationships in a Caribbean village." *Ethology and Sociobiology* 9: 335–69.

―――― and B. G. England (1995). "Childhood stress and family environment." *Current Anthropology* 36: 854–66.

―――― and B. G. England (1997). "The social economics of childhood glucocorticoid stress response and health." *American Journal of Physical Anthropology* 102: 33–53.

――――, R. Quinlan, et al. (1996). "Male-female differences in effects of parental absence on glucocorticoid stress response." *Human Nature* 7: 125–62.

Bibliography

Foley, W. A. (1991). *Anthropological Linguistics: An Introduction*. Oxford, Blackwell Publishers.

Gannon, D., and R. Holloway (1998). "Asymmetry of chimpanzee planum temporale: Humanlike pattern of Wernick's brain language area homolog." *Science* 279: 220–22.

Gibbs, N. (1998). The age of ritalin. *Time*. 152.

Gleason, J. (1987). Sex differences in parent-child interactions. *Language, Gender, and Sex in Comparative Perspective*. S. Philips, S. Steele, and C. Tanz. Cambridge, Cambridge University Press: 189–99.

Golinkoff, R. M., and K. Hirsh-Pasek (1999). *How Babies Talk*. New York, Dutton.

Gopnik, A., A. N. Meltzoff, and P. Kuhl (1999). *The Scientist in the Crib: Minds, Brains, and How Children Learn*. New York, William Morrow and Company.

Gosling, L. (1986). "Selective abortion of entire litters in the coypu: Adaptive control of offspring production in relation to quality and sex." *American Naturalist* 127: 772–95.

Gouzoules, S., H. Gouzoules, et al. (1984). "Rhesus monkey *(Macaca mulatta)* screams: Representational signalling in the recruitment of agonistic aid." *Animal Behaviour* 32: 182–93.

Habicht, J. P., C. Yarbrough, et al. (1974). "Height and weight standards for preschool children." *Lancet* 1: 611–15.

Harkness, S. (1990). "A cultural model for the acquisition of language: Implications for the innateness debate." *Developmental Psychobiology* 23: 727–40.

——— and C. M. Super (1997). "Why African children are so hard to test." *Annal of the New York Academy of Science* 285: 326–31.

Harrison, G. A., J. M. Tanner, et al. (1988). *Human Biology*. Oxford, Oxford University Press.

Hart, B., and T. R. Risley (1995). *Meaningful Differences in the Everyday Experience of Young American Children*. Baltimore, Paul H. Brookes.

Harvey, P. H., R. D. Martin, et al. (1987). Life histories in comparative perspective. *Primate Societies*. B. B. Smuts, D. L. Cheney, R. L. Seyfarth, R. W. Wrangham, and T. T. Strusaker. Chicago, University of Chicago Press: 181–96.

Bibliography

Hauser, M. D. (1997). *The Evolution of Communication.* Cambridge, M.I.T. Press.

Hawkes, K. (1998). "Grandmothering, menopause, and the evolution of human life histories." *Proceedings of the National Academy of Science* 95: 1–4.

———— (1999). "Hadza women's time allocation, offspring provisioning, and the evolution of long postmenopausal life spans." *Current Anthropology* 38: 551–77.

————, J. O'Connell, et al. (1995). "Hadza children's foraging; juvenile dependency, social arrangements, and mobility among hunter-gatherers." *Current Anthropology* 36: 688–700.

Humphries, S., J. Mack, et al. (1988). *A Century of Childhood.* London, Sidgwich and Jackson.

Isbell, L. A., and T. P. Young (1995). "Bipedalism and reduced group size: Alternative evolutionary responses to decreased resource availability." *Journal of Human Evolution* 30: 389–97.

James, A. (1998). From the child's point of view; issues in the social construction of childhood. *Biosocial Perspectives on Children.* C. Panter-Brick. Cambridge, Cambridge University Press: 45–65.

————, C. Jenks, et al. (1998). *Theorizing Childhood.* Cambridge, Polity Press.

Jenkins, C. L., A. K. Orr-Ewing, et al. (1984). "Cultural aspects of early childhood growth and nutrition among the Amele of lowland Papua New Guinea." *Ecology of Food and Nutrition* 14: 261–75.

Johnson, O. R. (1981). The socioeconomic context of child abuse and neglect in native South America. *Child Abuse and Neglect: Cross-Cultural Perspectives.* J. E. Korbin. Berkeley, University of California Press: 56–70.

Jolly, A. (2000). *Lucy's Legacy.* Cambridge, Harvard University Press.

Kantrowitz, B. (2000). Stop the insanity. *Newsweek.* July 8.

Kohlberg, L. (1981). *The Meaning and Measurement of Moral Development,* Heinz Werner Institute.

Korbin, J. E. (1981). *Child Abuse and Neglect: Cross-Cultural Perspectives.* Berkeley, University of California Press.

———— (1981). Introduction. *Child Abuse and Neglect: Cross-Cultural Perspectives.* J. E. Korbin. Berkeley, University of California Press: 1–12.

———— (1987). Child maltreatment in cross-cultural perspective: Vulnerable children and circumstances. *Child Abuse and Neglect: Biosocial Dimensions.* R. J. Gelles and J. B. Lancaster. New York, Aldine de Gruyter: 31–55.

Kramer, K. L. (1998). Variation in Children's Work Among Modern Maya Subsistence Agriculturalists. *Anthropology.* Albuquerque, University of New Mexico.

———— (in press) *Maya Children's Work. A Case Study in Subsistence Ecology and Family Labor Strategies.* Cambridge, Harvard University Press.

Kuczynski, L., C. Zahn-Waxler, et al. (1987). "Development and content of imitation in the second and third year of life." *Developmental Psychology* 23: 276–82.

Lancaster, J. B., and C. S. Lancaster (1983). Parental investment: The hominid adaptation. *How Humans Adapt.* D. J. Ortner. Washington, D.C., Smithsonian Institution Press: 33–65.

Lanhness, L. L. (1981). Child abuse and cultural values: The case of New Guinea. *Child Abuse and Neglect: Cross-Cultural Perspectives.* J. E. Korbin. Berkeley, University of California Press: 13–34.

Lasker, G. W. (1952). "Environmental growth factors and selective migration." *Human Biology* 24: 262–89.

Leach, P. (1989). *Your Baby and Child.* New York, Alfred A. Knopf.

Lee, P. C., P. Mayluf, et al. (1991). "Growth, weaning, and maternal investment from a comparative perspective." *Journal of the Zoological Society of London* 225: 99–114.

Lee, R. B. (1976). Introduction. *Kalahari Hunter-Gatherers.* R. B. Lee and I. deVore. Cambridge, Harvard University Press: 3–24.

LeVine, R. A. (1974). "Parental goals: A cross-cultural view." *Teachers College Record* 76: 226–39.

————, S. Dixon, et al. (1994). *Child Care and Culture: Lessons from Africa.* Cambridge, Cambridge University Press.

———— and B. B. LeVine (1963). Nyansongo: A Gusii Community in Kenya. *Six Cultures; Studies of Child Rearing.* B. B. Whiting. New York, John Wiley and Sons: 19–202.

Bibliography

Levy, R. I. (1996). Essential contrasts: Differences in parental ideas about learners and teaching in Tahiti and Nepal. *Parents' Cultural Belief Systems: The Origins, Expression and Consequences.* S. Harkness and C. M. Super. New York, Guilford Press: 123–42.

Lewis, C. C. (1995). *Educating Hearts and Minds.* Cambridge, Cambridge University Press.

Lewis, M., and J. Brooks-Gunn (1979). *Social Cognition and the Acquisition of Self.* New York, Plenum.

Lewis, T. (2000). Grandparents play a big part in grandchildren's lives. *The New York Times.* New York. January 4.

Lieberman, P. (1991). *Uniquely Human: The Evolution of Speech, Thought, and Selfless Behavior.* Cambridge, Harvard University Press.

Lovejoy, O. C. (1981). "The origin of man." *Science* 211: 341–50.

Maccoby, E. E. (1988). "Gender as a social category." *Developmental Psychobiology* 24: 755–65.

———— (1998). *The Two Sexes: Growing Up Apart, Growing Together.* Cambridge, Harvard University Press.

Martin, R. D. (1983). *Human brain evolution in an ecological context.* 52nd James Arthur Lecture, American Museum of Natural History.

McFarland Symington, M. (1987). "Sex ratio and matranl rank in wild spider monkeys: When daughters disperse." *Behavioral Ecology and Sociobiology* 20: 421–25.

Miller, G. (2000) *The Mating Mind: How Sexual Choice Shaped the Evolution of Human Nature.* New York, Doubleday.

Miller, S. Z., and B. Valman (1997). *Children's Medical Guide.* New York, DK Publishing.

Minturn, L., and J. T. Hitchcock (1963). The Rajputs of Khalapur, India. *Six Cultures: Studies of Child Rearing.* B. B. Whiting. New York, John Wiley and Sons: 207–361.

Mitani, J. C. (1985). "Gibbon song duets and intergroup spacing behavior." *Behaviour* 92: 59–96.

Bibliography

Morton, H. (1996). *Becoming Tongan: An Ethnography of Childhood.* Honolulu, University of Hawai'i Press.

Munroe, R. H., R. L. Munroe, et al. (1984). "Children's work in four cultures: Determinants and consequences." *American Anthropologist* 86: 369–79.

Mussen, P. H., J. J. Conger, et al. (1990). *Child Development and Personality.* New York, Harper & Row.

Nucci, L. P., and E. Turiel (1978). "Social interactions and the development of social concepts in preschool children." *Child Development* 49: 400–7.

Ochs, E., and B. B. Schieffelin (1984). Language acquisition and socialization. *Culture Theory: Essays on Mind, Self, and Emotion.* R. A. Schweder and R. A. LeVine. Cambridge, Cambridge University Press: 256–313.

Panter-Brick, C. (1997). "Seasonal growth patterns in rural Nepali children." *Human Biology* 24: 1–18.

——— (1998). Introduction: Biosocial research on children. *Biosocial Perspectives on Children.* C. Panter-Brick. Cambridge, Cambridge University Press: 1–9.

Peisner, E. S. (1989). To spare or not to spare the rod. *Child Development in Cultural Context.* J. Valsiner. Toronto, Hogrefe and Huber Publishers: 111–41.

Pereira, M. E., and L. Fairbanks (1993). *Juvenile Primates.* Oxford, Oxford University Press.

Pinker, S. (1994). *The Language Instinct.* New York, William Morrow and Co.

Postman, N. (1982). *The Disappearance of Childhood.* New York, Delacorte Press.

Rodman, P. S., and H. M. McHenry (1980). "Bioenergetics and the origin of hominid bipedalism." *American Journal of Physical Anthropology* 52: 103–6.

Rosenberg, K., and W. Trevethan (1995/96). "Bipedalism and human birth: The obstetrical dilemma revisited." *Evolutionary Anthropology* 4: 161–68.

Rosenberg, K. R. (1992). "The evolution of modern human birth." *Yearbook of Physical Anthropology* 35: 89–124.

Rosenthal, M. K. (1992). Nonparental child care in Israel: A cultural and historical perspective. *Child Care in Context: Cross-Cultural Perspectives.* M. E. Lamb, K. J. Sternberg, C. Hwang, and A. G. Broberg. Hillsdale, Lawrence Earlbaum: 305–30.

Sachs, A. (2000). When pills make sense. *Time.* March 20.

Sapolsky, R. M. (1994) *Why Zebras Don't Get Ulcers.* New York, W. H. Freeman.

Savage-Rumbaugh, E. S. (1986). *Ape Language; From Conditioned Response to Symbol.* New York, Columbia University Press.

Scheper-Hughes, N. (1992). *Death Without Weeping.* Berkeley, University of California Press.

Schieffelin, B. B. (1986). "Language socialization." *Annual Review of Anthropology* 15: 163–91.

———— (1990). *The Give and Take of Everyday Life.* Cambridge, Cambridge University Press.

Shapiro, H. L. (1939). *Migration and Environment.* Oxford, Oxford University Press.

Shelov, S. P. (1998). *Caring for Your Baby and Young Child.* New York, Bantam.

Sinclair, D. (1985). *Human Growth After Birth.* Oxford, Oxford University Press.

Small, M. F. (1995). *What's Love Got to Do with It? The Evolution of Human Mating.* New York, Anchor Books.

———— (1998). *Our Babies, Ourselves: How Biology and Culture Shape the Way We Parent.* New York, Anchor Books.

Smuts, B. B. (1985). *Sex and Friendship in Baboons.* New York, Aldine.

Takahashi, E. (1984). "Secular trends in milk consumption and growth in Japan." *Human Biology* 56: 427–37.

Tanner, J. M. (1990). *Fetus Into Man: Physical Growth from Conception to Maturity.* Cambridge, Harvard University Press.

Tobin, J. J., D. Y. H. Wu, et al. (1989). *Preschool in Three Cultures.* New Haven, Yale University Press.

Trivers, R. L., and D. E. Willard (1973). "Natural selection of parental ability to vary the sex ratio of offspring." *Science* 179: 90–91.

Turnbull, C. M. (1983). *The Human Cycle.* New York, Simon & Schuster.

Walker, A., and P. Shipman (1997). *The Wisdom of the Bones.* New York, Vintage.

Weisner, T. S., and R. Gallimore (1977). "My brother's keeper: child and sibling caretaking." *Current Anthropology* 18: 169–90.

Bibliography

Werner, E. E., and R. S. Smits (1989). *Vulnerable But Invincible: A Longitudinal Study of Resilient Children and Youth.* New York, Adams-Bannister-Cox.

White, B. (1975). The economic importance of children in a Javanese village. *Population and Social Organization.* M. Nag. The Hague, Moulton: 127–46.

Whiting, B. (1963). *Six Cultures: Studies of Child Rearing.* New York, John Wiley.

———— and J. Whiting (1975). *Children of Six Cultures.* Cambridge, Cambridge University Press.

———— and C. P. Edwards (1988). *Children of Different Worlds: The Formation of Social Behavior.* Cambridge, Harvard University Press.

Wilson, M., and M. Daly (1987). Risk of maltreatment of children living with stepparents. *Child Abuse and Neglect: Biosocial Dimensions.* R. J. Gelles and J. B. Lancaster. New York, Aldine de Gruyter: 215–32.

Woodburn, J. C. (1968). An introduction to Hadza ecology. *Man the Hunter.* R. B. Lee and I. DeVore. Chicago, Aldine: 49–55.

Wrangham, R. W., W. C. McGrew, et al. (1994). *Chimpanzee Cultures.* Cambridge, Harvard University Press.

Wynn, T. (1988). Tools and the evolution of human intelligence. *Machiavellian Intelligence: Social Expertise and the Evolution of Intellect in Monkeys, Apes, and Humans.* R. W. Byrne and A. Whiten. Oxford, Clarendon Press: 271–84.

Zeller, A. C. (1994). "A role for women in hominid evolution." *Man* 22: 528–57.

Acknowledgments

The chapters in this book skate across any number of subjects, and so I must first thank researchers in the fields of anatomy, physiology, neuroanatomy, child behavior, child psychology, and anthropology for the great work that forms the basis for this book.

Specifically, I thank Barry Bogin, Lee Cronk, Mark Flinn, Karen Kramer, and Catherine Panter-Brick for sharing their work with me and allowing me to interpret their studies. Amy Parish was gracious enough to share the story of her son's early days and allow me to write about them. In many cases, these researchers also sent me reprints that saved endless hours in the library searching out individual articles.

I also thank Adam Clark Arcadi for reading the chapter on language acquisition and giving me the great quote at the end of the book during one of our many fruitful discussions about parenting in America. Adam and I are parents who are also anthropologists, academics with a bent for yakking on and on about these big picture issues. Our presumed casual talks had a significant effect on this book and I am grateful to Adam for his time and wisdom.

I especially want to thank Mark Flinn, who allowed me to accompany him and his research team to Dominica. My visit there was enlightening. What a joy it was to see such a fine piece of ongoing anthropological research and to meet the wonderful people of Bwa Mawego, who have been active participants in this work.

I also thank several of my pals who were kind enough to ask about the progress on the book—Dede Hatch, Ann Jereb, Carol Terrizzi, Tom Terrizzi, Becky Rolfs. Guess what, I'm finished. And of course, to my "writer friends," I give profuse thanks and the usual free book. Mike May and Steve Mirsky continue to help me keep a level head during the business of writing.

Thanks also to my agent, Anne Sibbald at Janklow and Nesbitt, for continuing to be a supportive fan.

Roger Scholl, my editor at Doubleday, is the best editor a writer could have—his influence on this book has been felt from the proposal to the finished product. Our relationship continues to be one of the best aspects of this writing life.

Tim Merrick, as per usual, lived through the writing of this book, and the writing of so many magazine articles with so many different outcomes. And he did it with good cheer. As a parent, Tim also put many of the issues I wrote about in *Our Babies, Ourselves* into practice, and made sure I lived by my own words.

And most of all, I thank my daughter Francesca, who makes

writing this book, and everything else in my life, worth it. *Time* journalist Jill Smolowe once wrote what I think are the perfect words about parenting, and I repeat them here for Francesca. "I see you. I love you. I am yours and you are mine." This book is yours as well.

MEREDITH F. SMALL

Ithaca, N.Y.

July 2000

Index

Index

Index

nutrition and, 55
parenting and, 75–76
physical, 66, 112, 188
psychological, 66, 124, 189
stress and, 187–88
traditions and, 55
in United States, 67–68
Child homicide, 199, 200
Child labor, 26–27, 30, 67, 127
Child neglect, 204, 206, 207
"Child nurses," 28
Childhood, 14–15, 35–55
among Hadza people, 21–24
among San people, 18–21, 23, 24
definition of, 39
growth during, 44–48, 52. *See also*
Brain growth; Growth
in hunter-gatherer societies, 18–24,
50, 51, 215
as life cycle stage, 5, 6, 33, 38–39,
44–45, 52, 55, 216
pain during, 184–85
play in. *See* Play
stress during, 185–94
work in. *See* Chores; Work
Children/kids
activities of, 188, 226
adopted Romanian, 192
age of. *See* Age
of alcoholic parents, 207
brain growth in. *See* Brain growth
brain in adults *vs.*, 65
busy life of, 188, 226
child care by, 28, 29
coercion of, 206
with deformities, 204
enjoying, 228–29
exposure to other, 2, 94
family trauma and, 184
"favorite," 194–99
head size in, 64
health of, 184
of immigrants, 67, 130

knowledge of, 109–35
language acquisition by. *See*
Language acquisition
learning from other, 24–25, 150
of mentally ill parents, 207
resilience of, 206–9
at risk, 7, 27, 185, 199–207, 211
stress and, 185–94
thinking by, 110–21
Children's Medical Guide, 73
Chimpanzees, 53, 54, 115, 172
communication by, 79–80, 85,
87–88, 92
empathy in, 119–20
Chinese children, 97, 196
Chomsky, Noam, 88, 89, 90
Chores, 21, 30. *See also* Work
gender and, 173–74
for Gusii children, 128
for Hadza children, 23
school and, 133
for Western children, 27, 31–32, 218
Chromosomes, 164, 165–66, 167, 172
Circumcision, 177, 178, 179, 180, 203
Citizenship, 6, 14, 137–81, 143
Climate, 67–68, 69
Cognition, 7. *See also* Mental
development; Thinking
concept of, 111
symbolism in, 113–14
theories of, 121–24
Communication, 42, 77, 78–80, 86–87
Community, 19–20, 93, 130, 146, 150
Competition, 135, 149
Conflict, 140, 145, 149, 150
discipline and, 158
stress and, 190
Connection, 150, 170, 203
Cooperation, 13, 131
Cortex, 82–83
Cortisol, 61, 184, 187–92
Cronk, Lee, 88, 196–98

Index

Index

Environment
    of growth, 68–71
    language acquisition and, 92–96
    mental development and, 121
    social, 123
Epiphyses, 60
Estrogen, 61
Ethnicity, 141
Ethnography, 16–17, 31, 99–100, 148, 172, 184, 186
Europe, 30, 67, 186
Evolutionary biology, 2–3, 5, 31
    child abuse and, 199–200, 201, 206
    child development and, 123–24
    childhood and, 37–55
    and childhood pain, 184–85, 194
    "favorite" children and, 194, 199
    gender identity and, 171–72
    and kids at risk, 7, 185
    socialization and, 141, 142
    of speech, 85–88, 107
Expectations, 14, 28, 226
    child development and, 75–76
    gender roles and, 169
    parental scripts and, 139
    school and, 225
Experience, 43, 116, 123, 167
    biology vs., 89
    brain growth and, 66

Family, 133
    blended/reconstituted, 201–2
    composition of, 186, 191, 200
    discipline and, 158
    language acquisition and, 93–94
    morality and, 146
    nuclear vs. extended, 139, 193, 205, 213–17
    stress and, 188, 193, 194
Family Life 1st, 226

Family trauma, 69, 184, 190–92, 193, 206–9
Fat cells, 59, 69
Fathers
    in Caribbean, 186
    Kipsigis, 126
    language and, 105
    stress and, 191
    in Trinidad, 185
Fatigue, 191
"Favorite" children, 194–99
Fear of punishment, 144, 145
Fear of strangers, 74
Feelings, 118–21, 146. See also
        Emotions; Empathy; Sympathy
Fertility/birthrate, 223, 227, 228
Fetus. See also Prenatal life
    abortion of, 195
    bone growth in, 59
    male vs. female, 60
Flinn, Mark, 184, 185–94, 200
"Folklore," 90
Food. See also Eating; Nutrition
    child abuse and, 205
    childhood and, 48
    gender and, 175
    growth and, 70–71
    language development and, 51
    stress and, 186, 189
    weaning and, 47, 48, 50
French language, 97
Freud, Sigmund, 122
Freudian models, 29

Games, 149, 152, 180
Garifuna people, 30
Gates, Bill, 212
Gender roles, 7, 30, 163, 169, 173. See
        also Boys; Gender/sex; Girls
    among Gusii people, 177–79

Index

Index

Hormones, 61–62, 165–66, 167
   resilience and, 208
   stress and, 187, 189. *See also* Cortisol
Household/domestic work, 29–32, 50,
   128, 173–74, 218
   by Gusii children, 179, 223
   by Mbuti pygmies, 149
Hrdy, Sarah Blaffer, 196
Human growth hormone, 61
Human rights, 159
Humans. *See also* Animals, nonhuman *vs.*
   human; Primates, human
   as animals, 38, 40–43, 225
   apes *vs.*, 47
   environment and, 122
   evolution of, 41–42, 52–53, 214–15
   gender and, 172
   growth in. *See* Brain growth;
   Growth
   interbirth intervals for apes *vs.*,
   48–49
   reproduction among ancestral, 51, 52
   talking by, 90, 107. *See also*
   Communication; Language
   acquisition; Speech
Hungarian Gypsies, 197
Hunter-gatherers, 17–24, 50, 51, 148,
   214, 215
   punishment among, 159
   tool use by, 87
Hypothalamus, 61

Identity, 141–42, 152
   gender and, 163, 171
   language and, 104
   morality and, 146
Illegitimacy, 204
Imagination, 114, 149
Imitation, 79, 114–15, 116, 132, 134,
   149, 176, 222

Immersion, 139, 149
Immigrants, children of, 67, 130
Immune system, 187, 188, 191
Immunization, 212
Immunoglobulin, stress and, 184
Independence, 13, 76, 125–26, 152, 227
   isolation and, 217
   obedience *vs.*, 157–58
   socialization and, 148
   stress and, 194
India, 173, 174, 175–77, 215–16
   infanticide in, 196
Individualism, 75
Infant mortality, 204, 211, 212
Infanticide, 195, 196, 198, 204
Inhibition, 166
Initiation, 177, 179
"Innatist" approach, 88–89
"Insight," 115–16
Intellectual development, 66
Intelligence
   culture and, 126–27
   imitation and, 114–15
   self-expression and, 118, 127
Interactions, 42, 76, 133. *See also*
   Interpersonal attachments;
   Interpersonal skills; Socialization;
   Socializing
   adult-child. *See* Adult-child
   interactions
   among Mbuti pygmies, 149, 150
   among San people, 20
   and evolution of speech, 86
   gender and, 171
   language acquisition and, 92
   morality and, 145
   in preschool, 12
   socialization and, 138, 139
   stress and family, 191
   in Western culture, 32
Interbirth interval, 48–49, 50
Interpersonal attachments, 29

Index

Index

by imitation, 114–15, 116, 132. *See also* Imitation
intelligence and, 127
in Khalapur, India, 176
in language acquisition, 88–89, 90, 91, 103
lifelong, 134–35
of parenting skills, 28
"participatory," 129
school and, 127, 129–33, 134, 135, 221. *See also* Preschool; School
LeVine, Robert, 128–29, 132–33, 147–48, 177, 223
LeVine, Sarah, 147
Levy, Robert, 128
Lewis, Catherine, 131
Life cycle
childhood in, 5, 6, 33, 38–39, 44–45, 52, 55, 216
maturity in, 63
of Mbuti pygmies, 149
Linguistic relativism, 99
Listening/hearing, 80–85
Little, Molly, 11
Locke, John, 154
Logoli people, 30

Maasai, 197
Maccoby, Eleanor, 168, 169, 171
Madagascar, 15
Magnetic resonance imaging (MRI), 84
Malnutrition, 69
Martin, R. D., 53
Materialism, 217–18
Maturity/maturation, 61, 63, 66, 187, 192
Mayan people, 25–26, 67
Mbuti pygmies, 148–50, 152, 159
McKenna, James, 226
Mead, Margaret, 16

Melatonin, 61
Meltzoff, Andrew, 124
Memory, 116
Mental development, 110, 111–35
empathy and, 120–21
physical entwined with, 112
Merrick, Susan Childs, 10
Metabolism, 65, 169, 225
Mexicans, 67, 174
Mexico, 25–26, 173
Middle class, 4, 32, 94, 100–101, 123, 157, 188
Mixed-age groups, 20, 23, 24, 25, 29, 94–95, 133
among Mbuti pygmies, 149
among Tongan people, 152
Monkeys, 5, 35–37
communication by, 78
concept of self in, 117–18
"theory of mind" in, 117
Montbeillard, Philibert Geréneau de, 66
Moral/good citizens, 6, 14, 137, 138, 143–46, 153, 155–56
Morton, Helen, 150–52
"Motherese," 91
Mothers, 217
in Caribbean, 186
child abuse and, 200, 205–6
gender typing and, 173
Hadza, 215
imitation of, 114
infant mortality and, 204
in Khalapur, India, 177
Kipsigis, 126
language and, 105
school and, 133
stress and, 191
Tongan, 151
MRI. *See* Magnetic resonance imaging (MRI)
Mukogodo people, 197–98
Munroe, Ruth and Robert, 29–30

Index

Muscle growth, 58, 59, 61
Mylination, 66

Namibia, 18
Nanny, 139
Nature vs. nurture, 89, 122
Nepal, 68
Nerve cells, 59
Neurons, 64–65
New Guinea, 70, 101, 205
Newar people, 30
Nutrition. *See also* Eating; Food
  bone growth and, 60
  breast milk and, 70
  child development and, 55
  growth and, 60, 67, 69–71
  over-, 69
  stress and, 186, 190
  vs. other factors in growth, 69

Obedience, 157–58, 177, 223
Obesity, 69
Observation, 116, 176
Ochs, Elinor, 99, 101
Orangutans, 53, 115
Orphans, 192, 212
Our Babies, Ourselves, 2, 3, 18

Pacific islands, 151, 158, 159
Pakistan, 196
Papua New Guinea, 70
Parenting, 1–2, 227–29
  child development and, 75–76
  in Israel, 129–30

philosophy of, 154–55, 158
scripts for, 139–40, 154, 158
trade-offs in, 7, 212–13
Parents. *See also* Caretakers
  alcoholic/mentally ill, 207
  expectations of, 76. *See also*
    Expectations
  fathers *vs.* mothers as, 105
  gender and, 167, 170–71
  goals of, 76
  language and, 105
  single, 193, 212, 216
Parish, Amy, 161–62
"Participatory learning," 129
Pediatricians, 2, 4, 71, 72, 81
Peer groups, 32
  among Mbuti pygmies, 149
  gender and, 168–69
  stress and, 188
  vs. mixed-age, 20, 24, 25
Peisner, Ellen, 155
Performance anxiety, 188
Personality, 141
  culture and, 16, 29
  discipline and, 158
  stress and, 188, 192
Personality tests, 126–27
Peru, 205
Philippines, 173
Phonemes, 80, 81, 96
Physical development, 66
  mental entwined with, 112
  stress and, 188
Physical punishment
  child abuse and, 153, 157
  of Pacific island children, 158, 159
  stress and, 190
  of Tongan children, 152–53, 158
Piaget, Jean, 121–22
Pilaga, 205–6
Pinker, Stephen, 90
Piri people, 127–28, 134
Pituitary gland, 61

Index

Index

Index

Index